Digicrimination – Those are the Go

H. Okan Tansu

Digicrimination –
Those are the Good Times

A New Type of Discrimination
That Came with Digitization

PETER LANG

Bibliographic information published by die Deutsche Nationalbibliothek
The Deutsche Nationalbibliothek lists this publication in the Deutsche
Nationalbibliografie; detailed bibliographic data is available on the
Internet at http://dnb.d-nb.de.

Library of Congress Cataloging-in-Publication Data
A CIP catalog record for this book has been applied at the
Library of Congress.

Cover illustration: © iStock.com/muratsenel

ISBN 978-3-631-73508-4 (Print)
E-ISBN 978-3-631-73509-1 (E-PDF)
E-ISBN 978-3-631-73510-7 (EPUB)
E-ISBN 978-3-631-73511-4 (MOBI)
DOI 10.3726/b11828

© Peter Lang GmbH
International Academic Publishers
Berlin 2018
All rights reserved.

Peter Lang – Berlin · Bern · Bruxelles · New York ·
Oxford · Warszawa · Wien

This publication has been peer reviewed

www.peterlang.com

Preface

I met Okan right after elementary school. We studied together till the end of high school. While our personal interests carried us away in different ways -positive sciences for me and social sciences for him-, we both stayed in the academic world. I am now experiencing the happiness of reading a book that he wrote about a technological subject which touched the lives of all of us and share a few sentences about it with the point of view by a social scientist.

I think the internet is the indispensable part of the 21st century. I am not saying this because it was invented for easier communication among people of science in the institution where I am now working on http(www) and the concept of the internet, at CERN and in different nations. If a question as "which is worse, no electricity or no internet?" can be asked, there is no need for debate. Moreover, if tactics of "my mobile phone battery should stay at 100%, let us charge the power-bank" are common against the possibility of a power cut, it is already too late to ask the question "is the digital world forced upon us?".

Of course, everything happened so fast. In the recent past, we were filling buckets and bathtubs against the possibility of a water cut-off. However, let us not forget that the generation before us was storing flour and salt in their houses for "there might be a war." They would ask "can you use a fax machine, a photocopy machine?" in job interviews in the past and we would laugh. Then it became fashionable to write "I can use MS Word, MS Excel" in resumés. I still see this in some applications. They can use MS Office! It would be discrimination to say that I put the resumés of those who include this information at the bottom of the pile, right? Nevertheless, I do, because this does not give me additional information about them. If I find my father, to whom I gave an iPad that he never saw before in the morning, browsing internet pages by himself in the evening, young applicants should learn to express their diversity in other forms. Improvement is change, but the change is now faster.

I accept that my colleagues at CERN and I are not only living in technology, but also lead its advancement and even innovation. Just like people living among trees not being able to see the forest, while living in a digital and virtual world we invented, we usually ignored or even failed to notice the social influence of these developments. Does the digital world bring discrimination? Of course it does. Is a person with an iPhone 7 the same as another who is still using their Nokia from the time of Noah? The former is carrying beautiful photographs in their pocket; the other can only call home. If they want, they can carry a camera in the other pocket.

Think about it. We would listen to the BBC to receive the news from any place in the world. We now have reporters who are able to transmit the news to us in any place and time. We are not even paying them. They make efforts to share their information with us, only for a little "like". Of course, we have accumulated enough experience in these virtual ecosystems to learn not to trust everything that is written. Is this not the new form of the sentence "do not believe the words of strangers" that our parents used before sending us to school? Or the saying "look at the other side of the medallion before making a decision."

There are also situations where digitization reduces or even eliminates discrimination. Think about multinational corporations. They have been selling the same product with different prices in different countries for years. They invented a concept called "bon pour l'Orient". They sent the products that Europeans did not or would not buy to the Middle East and Balkans. Is it possible now? If you have an internet connection, never! If not, ask your neighbor to look it up, and learn about how much that nice cabinet you bought for 1000 TL from the store costs in its country of origin. Make sure to check not only the prices in two different stores in the same streets, but also those in two different continents. Then be thankful for people who provided you with this opportunity. This ease of distribution of information and easy access to information, I think, will lead to transformations in systems that have been taught to us as correct since our childhood. Especially about government. Why would societies still need representatives? As long as there is working software, anyone can express their opinion for a new idea, just as in the Ancient Greek agoras. The only difference is that, instead of gathering physically in that area, we will speak and discuss in the virtual square. Such a system will eliminate discrimination, which has unfortunately been experienced in societies in recent years. The only condition is that the programmers of such a software do not allow discrimination.

Okan thought about these problems for us and was able to see the entire forest by looking from on top of Mount Ağrı calmly. This is why his book concerns both those living as one with digital technology and those who would claim that they are or will be strangers to the subject entirely. Okan introduces us to ideas that we have not heard of yet, or those we have heard of but ignored. Abbreviations like "ICTIQ, CBD" and new concepts such as "Digital Schizophrenia, Screen Addiction, Digitally Ignorant, Neuromarketing" come alive with Okan's absorbing and fun language full of examples from his own experiences. Other perks of the book include historical connections with analogies from Ancient Greece to some recent concepts (such as addictive computer games that are nightmares for some parents), and clues that he provides for those who want to read about the details of a subject.

Does the digital world only bring beauty? Of course not. We are becoming more hunchbacked, astigmatic and obese every day. However, these changes will maybe help us survive in the near future in our increasingly polluted world. Maybe we will have to live in tiny boxes. Maybe we will have aquarium cities because of air pollution, or we will resort to planets without oxygen. Maybe only the fittest will survive. On the other hand, I agree with those who say, "our world is still beautiful, let us cherish it" too. Go out, travel, utilize the opportunities of technology. While doing this, however, do not forget about those who cannot utilize technology as much as you do. Instead of choosing your accommodation on *booking.com* or *Airbnb*, go to a town and ask "where is the travelers' inn?" If you are as fortunate as me, you will eat a superb chicken dish prepared by the cutest eighty-year-old couple ever, drink the best wines and have a great sleep afterwards.

When luck is taken into account, it becomes more difficult to have a projection about the future. Especially due to various factors that are impossible to measure in social sciences, it is more difficult to make predictions about social issues. This may be why Okan made his predictions by starting with issues that we are able to see with their potential directions such as transportation or energy, and thought about how these will change social life. This methodology makes his predictions more realistic and credible. The main issue questioned in the book is, what is the price of keeping one's distance from the virtual world? What is it today and what will it be tomorrow? The word "digicrimination" (digital discrimination) that was invented by the author is exactly the answer to these questions. If the price of keeping away from the digital world or not being able to internalize the concept entirely is being late for dinner, having chosen a noisy hotel or sold fewer products today, what will it be tomorrow? Hence, I would want this book to be read by everyone, but especially by our educators and bureaucrats who will shape the future, and I would recommend such people to accept this book as a reference. This is how generations that are able to overcome digital discrimination will be created and we can take our place among leading countries in the 21st century.

Gökhan Ünel,
CERN,
European Organization for Nuclear Research,
Geneva

About the author

Born in 1968, Okan Tanşu, completed his high school studies in 1988 at Saint Joseph French High School in Istanbul. Then he got his University Degree at the Institut d'Etudes Politiques Istanbul Filiale in Political Sciences and Communication.

In 1994 he began his carrier as an academic and got his master's degree in Communication and Informatics with the thesis he wrote on Corporate Satellite Communication System management and Türksat. In 2000, he completed his PhD studies in the International Relations department where he received his doctoral degree with a thesis on 21st century conflict areas and informatics. In 2001 he became the vice dean of the Faculty of Communication at Istanbul Bilgi University. After lecturing at Istanbul Bilgi University for more than 15 years on different fields of communication like Sports, Technology and Political Economy, he moved to Germany in 2015. Since then, he has been lecturing in different universities in Hamburg.

Okan Tanşu, alongside his academic career, also owns a communication consultancy company, Kano, which delivers consultancy for strategic communication, marketing communication, and corporate communication, effective discourse and content providing services, sensory and emotive material composing.

For Şenay, Melisa and Meyra

Contents

Introduction

I started writing this book in 2002 with the main purpose of creating content that was focused on the world of informatics. However, I had to leave it aside due to various reasons. The developments in the fields related to the content of the book not only led to loss of topicality in some sections, but also necessitated addition of new sections. Finally, I was able to finish this work that discusses what the Age of Information has brought about from a general perspective. While this book discusses what is known about the digital world from a different perspective and tries to present the mistakes made in the transition to the Age of Information, the new technological ecosystem we will face in future times and what needs to be done, it also includes a set of ideas towards making our rapidly and overwhelmingly changing lives and lifestyles more comprehensible.

Without a doubt, information is a phenomenon whose importance has been known throughout history. Is the Chinese General Sun Tzu, who shared his thoughts on "superiority of those who have information" in his work named *The Art of War*, produced two thousand and five hundred years ago, still not right even today?[1] Likewise, the stinginess of people who have information in sharing it, as mentioned in the book *The Name of the Rose* by Umberto Eco, the approach of seeing this possession as a superiority, is still valid today to an extent it maybe never was before.

Of course, it is crucial to define and be able to understand the age we are living in, especially for being able to make inferences about social relationships. As we have heard hundreds and even thousands of times, many define the age we are living in as the Age of Information, while calling our society the Information Society. What do Age of Information and Information Society mean? As Daniel D. Loader wrote in his work entitled *Cyberspace Divide, Equality* back in 1998, "an economic and social set of new paradigms and values that reshape the time and space dimensions that we live in, interact with and work in"[2]. This statement is a little bit complicated to understand, one could say. More clearly, a society and an era where creation, distribution, sharing, storage and manipulation of information have become the most economically and culturally significant functions.

---

1   Griffith, S. B. (1982). *Sun tzu the art of war: translated and with an introduction.* London: Oxford University Press.
2   Loader, B. D. (2006). Cyberspace divide: equality, agency and policy in the information society. London: Routledge., p. 3.

In summary, an environment where information has a corresponding monetary value and can be sold.

The main characteristic that distinguishes the Information Society from others is that the fundamental building block of the economy is not industry or agriculture but information. Speaking in terms of production, the tools of production in the Information Society are not constituted by turning laths or wooden plows, but smartphones or computers.

It is, of course, very important to define the era we are living in and the period we are passing through. While the comments of various authors, academics, theoreticians and scientists such as Marshall McLuhan, Daniel Bell and most importantly and especially Alvin Toffler on the Information Society have become a point of reference for this book and shed light on it, they are not our main subject.[3]

The phenomenon we are experiencing today is accepted as the third Information Revolution in the history of humanity after the inventions of writing and the printing press. While it became possible to store information in the first and multiply and distribute in in the second, the charm of the third Information Revolution that is based on speed, creating a revolution that is different from the others, with much broader and deeper effects.

If the history of humanity were written again in a short and concise way it might be described as a journey from data to information, information to knowledge, and knowledge to expertise. A statement such as "throughout history, as the techniques and technologies that process information changed and developed, a great revolution took place in the name of humanity" would definitely not be false. Revolution means something different for different people. For some, the effects of revolution should be noticeably large, fast and deep. For others, revolution may be defined as complete change in the dominant lifestyles of societies. Regardless of the perspective we take here, the process of digitization of information that started with 1980 is a great and unprecedented revolution. The effects of this revolution are noticeable large, broad, widespread, and blunt enough to change lifestyles from scratch.

In addition to information, the history of humanity also witnessed revolutions in the field of communication where information plays the leading role. The basis of information, coding information and solving that code, has been interpreted in different ways. This interpretation, of course, was shaped on the basis of the means one has and technology, while being blended to appeal to the five senses of humankind. How and in what framework communication would be used was

---

3   Toffler, A. (1980). The third wave. New York: William Morrow.

determined by the lifestyles of society. The combination of technology and communication in the 21st century and the synergy it created forced all relationships that were defined beyond lifestyles in society to change completely. The relationships of student-school, customer-firm, citizen-state and various others started to be redefined with the results of informatics and information technologies. Such an effective and dominant change brought about by technology was an unprecedented case in the history of humankind. Therefore, some approaches defined the position of information in the center of our lives via information and communication technologies as the Age of Information.

I think that the top factor that makes this revolution very important among others is digitization. We owe it to the simple binary system that we are able to transfer all information, all data and knowledge created, sounds and visuals into the electronic environment and represent the information in question with 0s and 1s. Once the information and data were converted into 0s and 1s, devices that were able to code all the data mentioned above in the *binary* system and decode these when needed, and the infrastructure that is suitable for this, allowed the flow of this information to happen at the speed of electricity. With the prefix "e" that we constantly encounter, it became visible that information transferred to the electronic environment, a process or a situation was digital and electronically available: for example, e-mail, e-commerce, e-banking. After a point, this prefix became so widespread that it lost its significance and privilege, and it was no longer seen as worth using.

Talking about speed, one of the elements that has made technology and communication indispensably and revolutionarily qualified is speed. The concept of speed referred to fast travel, exchange of information and the temporal size of communication that included information; however, at the same time, it has been used towards processing powers of technological hardware and software. On the other hand, this speed was interpreted as renewal of technology and aging of a product initially considered as an innovation. I have occasionally mentioned the social effects created by this speed in the book, but of course, due to the difference between real life and the perception of speed created by technology, those who were not able to adapt to this situation found it difficult to find a place for themselves in the world after the Information Revolution.

This leap, taken in terms of technology, naturally required a transformation towards the prevalent usage of technology. In this context, the first factor in the prevalence of information and communication technologies was that they are easily usable and accessible by everyone. In 1980s, knowledge of a complicated programming language was necessary to be able to communicate with computers.

It was not possible to introduce the desired commands into computers without knowing the specific language. In a short time, like a decade, the way to easy usage was paved after the prevalence of user-friendly interfaces following the transformation of communication with computers into firstly a visual and then a tactile context. Thus, while communication tools turned into devices that were easily purchasable by billions, conveniently priced and easy to use, what these devices were able to do emerged as a field of development.

The second leap, again in this context, took place when personal and public computers were connected to each other via the platform called the internet. The information that was shared triggered the revolution. In my opinion, no one predicted or hoped for such an outcome at first. The synergy created by easy usage of software and hardware via the internet led to the birth of the Information Revolution. The introduction of the internet was not sufficient. In the initial years, it was troublesome to to connect to the internet over analog lines and achieve connectivity. In time, the connection infrastructure was updated, and it was brought up to a state that could respond to fast connections. This led to the opportunity for easy access to the internet by everyone. In the following stage, wireless internet emerged – and the infrastructure for it would become prevalent and independent of geographical constraints with the help of current projects. Naturally, ease of mobility came about after restrictions such as cables, dial-up lines and similar limitations were eliminated. While it seems like the most natural and optimal situation right now, in comparison to twenty years ago, it was a revolution by itself in terms of access to information. With the prevalence of wireless connections and audio and video conversations easily taking place on these networks, telecommunication firms that provide telephone lines as we know them and services related to these will be history.

Not too long, but about a hundred years ago, communication and telecommunication were privileges held only by certain individuals and a certain class of people. This privilege was not even more than a process that lasted for months. As a result of the developments mentioned above, after communication and telecommunication were no longer privileges, the great acceleration and wave of information shared on a personal level emerged in addition to the information shared in the public, commercial and macro areas. In addition to global communication coming down to a personal level, the affordable, fast and easy nature of communication for everyone became another factor that, once again, triggered the revolution.

Information and communication technologies are considered by many people to be limited to computers and the internet. I am not one of those people. In my view, the characteristics that make information and communication technologies uniquely significant are speed of accessing information and mobility. Calling the devices that we use while listening to music, telecommunication, showing up on social media, finding an address, listening to the radio or watching TV "phone", "computer, etc." and limiting these opportunities by concepts, in my opinion, is a shallow approach.

The speed of communication, commodification of information, access to the internet, transformation in telecommunication… As a result of these and dozens of revolutionary developments that may be included in this list, our lifestyles reached another order on a global level. Discussing this order with all of its details is, of course, not possible. On the other hand, it is possible to make predictions about the future by establishing evaluations. Today, we are discussing a revolution that started twenty-five years ago, but this does not mean this revolution has ended. Still, there is the same question on every level: well, what will happen next?

In this context, in the first part of the book, I discuss the changes we encountered in the last twenty-five years, focused on the difference the emerging revolution made in our lives, and tried to approach the social transformation created by this difference. In the second part, I discussed how some developments that I think will mark the next decade, and will reshape society and redefine relationships.

Section 1. Adapt and make your life easier

Bond... James Bond. The famous line of the famous movie. While the movie is filled with much action, espionage and many surreal scenes, the most important part of this movie for many technology enthusiasts is the scene where he is presented in a special laboratory with technological toys which he tries before leaving for a job. Automobiles with multiple functions at the press of a button, motorcycles, multi-function pens, cufflinks, tie clips... All of these are technological toys that make one say "wow!" Another cult screen masterpiece is *Star Trek*, with the famous line "Beam me up Scotty!" Is beaming not the most significant and impressive technology in this series? Which of us who has watched the series/movie did not dream of beaming in real life? Especially in childhood, which of us was not influenced by these advanced technologies? Scripts that are filled with time travel, flying, beaming, on-screen cases of all the dreams of humankind... The list can be made longer. While these scenes seem like the products of the world of entertainment, they create a feeling in all viewers that is similar to a feeling of a child desiring to own a toy. Thus these exciting movies and TV series have always been followed with passion. It is worth the world to have the means to be able to possess that technology and use it, and dream about it.

When we watch the not much older, but just 30-year-old versions of these movies, we see that most of the technologies that could not even be dreamt of in those times have already entered our lives and many have even already left us. For example, there is definitely truth in the idea that the design of Motorola flip phones was inspired by the communication devices in the series *Star Trek*, and therefore, it was the mobile phone design most preferred by American consumers for a long time.

In addition to all these, we are paying too little attention to how this process has affected our social life and the relationships that surround us. In this book, I discuss how technology reshapes our daily life cycle and social relationships at the same time as it changes our lives.

High school friendships are important. People attending the same high school start to grow similar to each other in a mental sense as they pass through years of the same type of education and the same culture, even if they come from different social backgrounds and families. Maybe because of the longing for good memories shared in those years, we want to gather with our high school friends at different periods of life and spend good times with them just like back in the old days. Even if we have moved in different directions and established our lives with different jobs and relationships as people who are almost produced by the same factory during a period of our lives…

I am also one of the people who frequently spend time with their high school friends although so many years have passed since graduation. I think this habit of mine comes from my high school's established history of one hundred and fifty years, and the close friendship bonds among graduates of traditional French high schools, rather than the longing I feel towards the past. This habit of mine is still ongoing despite the fact that I have been living abroad for some time. Yet of course the digital world, new technologies and daily usage of these also affect me and my friends.

Not long but only a few months ago, with two friends of mine from high school, we booked a time to watch the Euro League together and made a travel plan. We decided to gather in Berlin over the weekend when the finals would be held, watch the games and have a small reunion. As I am living in Germany, the general aspects of the organization were left to me.

Firstly, after taking on the job of planning, I connected to the internet and I looked for tickets to the games we planned to watch. I did not stop after comparing ticket prices on different websites, but I also checked the appearance of the court where games would be played as well as the seating area, and the position of our seats on a website that previously published a 360° view of the court. We bought the tickets after gathering over video conversations over the internet with the friends to discuss the details I collected.

The place we would stay in Berlin was next. The process went on, yet again, with the research we carried out on the internet. We used Google Maps to find the area that was the closest to the Fan-Zone, the sports hall and other activities. We determined a suitable area and started to evaluate the hotels. In the meantime, in addition to checking the price, I particularly read the comments of people who had previously stayed in these hotels. As the profiles of commenters also provided information on their lifestyles, I listed the most suitable hotels by considering the comments I found reliable and shared them with my friends. We compared the information with the information of another friend who conducted similar research and finalized the hotel selection.

When it came to transportation, I bought the departure tickets from the mobile application of Deutsche Bahn, which is the international railway administration of Germany. Then I downloaded the applications that would make our lives easier in Berlin on my phone. I did whatever I could in order to call a cab, plan subway trips, be able to book a place in the most popular locations s in the city, and in summary, to utilize our time in the best way possible without wasting time with formalities in the limited period we would spend there. After all, most of the applications I downloaded on my phone required neither a document nor an extra bureaucratic process.

> I looked at *booking.com* for hotels, and *tripadvisor.com* for assessments and comments. We used Skype for video calls. These are, of course, top options among dozens of other applications and platforms that have similar functions. The desired outcome may be achieved with similar applications in different countries and segments.

I know many of you are wondering why I included so many details for all these processes I went through for a vacation. After all, you might be repeating the same processes before travelling. Today, all these applications can be used easily and comfortably by large masses. In other words, there is no original aspect to carrying out the processes I mentioned above in the digital environment. Then, why did I include these details? Let me tell you.

We finished this travel planning process for which I provided so many details for fun, and the day we met finally arrived. I met the two high school friends whom I thought were products of the same system and shared similar lifestyles and views with me. After staying in Hamburg for a night, we went to Berlin next day with a train and went on our way to go to the hotel we booked. When we needed a cab to leave the train station, we contacted a car with the application I previously downloaded on my phone just to try, even though there were a lot of taxis in front of the station. As we completed everything via the internet before, we just got our room keys when we arrived at the hotel. We did not feel any unfamiliarity as we had previously checked the photos of the rooms. There were no surprises. In short, everything was going like clockwork. When we had settled into our hotel and the time to enjoy Berlin arrived, everyone had a different idea. This is why we scattered around different parts of the city before regrouping to have dinner. Right when we left each other, we started to experience the phenomenon that everyone utilized the digital world in a different way.

In the evening, when the time to meet arrived, I called a cab with the application on my phone again and went on my way. I opened the navigation application on my phone while moving in the traffic and hoped to prevent the worldwide traditional activity of cab drivers of making the journey longer for tourists and earning more. This may be the simplest benefit of being familiar with applications. When we arrived at the restaurant, I showed the employee the confirmation number sent to my phone by the reservation application. We were not names but a number for the restaurant employee, but the important thing was the result.

Without waiting, they accompanied us and directed us to our table. While waiting for our third friend, I noticed that I did not feel like a stranger as I spent a considerable amount of time on the website of the restaurant. It was as if I were a regular. I did not even go further than skimming the menu.

When our friend did not show up at the time we agreed upon, we decided to call him. Our friend said he was late because he could not find any cabs anywhere, but were on his way after finding one with difficulty. When asked again, I shared my location for the address on WhatsApp. While we thought he would arrive soon, he complained about going to another place with a similar name by mistake. It was the cab driver's fault. It would take even more time to find another cab and reach the restaurant. This was not the last of the problems. Then I was called from the door of the restaurant. Our names were provided, but our friend was not allowed to enter as the restaurant employee worked only with reservation numbers and did not recognize our names. As a result, our meeting at the table as three people took place with almost an hour's delay.

Über and similar applications gained a lot of attention especially as alternatives to cabs at first. However, they later faced prohibition in various countries due to issues of taxing, customer complaints, or unfair competition. In my view such applications will probably not disappear but will lose their initial appeal due to stricter regulations or they will need to transform into a different form of service.

While we were finally starting to have our meal, I also started to think. Are things like downloading a few applications, browsing through websites and utilizing the skills of a smartphone as much as possible so effective in organizing the flow of our affairs in real life? Would they create this much difference in the lifestyles of friends with similar values? Yet we graduated from the school with the same information and manners, and we were still sharing most of these. It was certain that there were also no social, emotional or other criteria of intelligence difference among us. However, despite this, while some of us were able to easily manage the flow of life, others were deprived of this. Then, maybe, we were facing yet another imposition by the digital world. In other words, the digitalized world was whispering to us; adapt, *or make your life harder.*

This and similar experiences led me to deepen my studies on how digitization affects our lives. This simple example on how digitization and the Information Revolution affect us is, of course, related to the fun part of life. If we experienced in a much more vital environment, such as a hospital, who knows what the results would be… The digital revolution did not only change the dynamics of various sectors we are used to in as short a time as a few decades, but it also led to the emergence of new lines of work. Also considering our story, we may easily argue that one of the sectors that were forced to change their ways of conducting business is tourism. To provide more details, hotel selection is no longer a lottery as it was twenty years ago. The website of a hotel, whatever its digital content is, plays an important role for its selection for accommodation. Moreover, in addition to high resolution photographs, videos, maps and 360-degree interactive images have become almost indispensable for a hotel's website. In this case, the desire to leave nothing to surprise in new consumer behavior led to a complete redefinition of the field of hotel management. It had become possible to reach tangible and intangible criteria for hotel selection via the digital world. If the organization and narrative of the website of a hotel are supported by visuals and videos that make it special and different, it is now very easy to have an idea about its actual conditions. It is even possible to support these ideas by applications such as "Google Street View". On the other hand, we may reach information about special need services, disabled access, child-friendliness, noisiness of the rooms, smell, lighting, size and view by accessing the opinions of people who previously stayed there. In other words, the detailed comments, criticisms, and notifications left by people who previously visited the hotel have become important factors in hotel selection. Additionally, in an environment where studies have reported that the cost of achieving existing customer loyalty and keeping those customers is much higher than the cost of gaining new customers, the experiences shared by customers in relation to their stay carry great importance for both existing and potential customers. Then what are customers who do not have these tangible and intangible changes, those who are not familiar with informatics, or those who cannot utilize the benefits of the digital world for any reason going to do? Or, if we evaluate the same example from a different perspective, what are the chances of hotels that do not create their websites with the features I mentioned above in this environment of competition? Does this situation, which is different from the discrimination that we are used to in our societies, not leave us with a new sort of discrimination?

Events in the digital world created an extraordinary revolution with a geo-metric increase, one that surpassed the projections regarding the post-industrial world by the prominent sociologist Daniel Bell. In the late 1990s, there were still several thinkers who thought that the developments in informatics were not a revolution but just a change. Yet, today, there is already a consensus that this change is a revolution. This was first mentioned by Daniel Bell.[4]

---

4   Daniel Bell, The Coming of Post-Industrial Society: A Venture in Social Forecasting, NY, Basic Books, 1973.

> Daniel Bell made highly interesting predictions about the Information Society of the 2000s in the book *The Coming of Post-Industrial Society*. This book is in my list of what should be read to understand our time.

According to many, the dimensions of this revolution are still limited to the internet, smartphones, social media posts and advanced video games. However, considering the policies followed and strategic decisions made in various fields, it can be understood that a large part of society has not yet comprehended the significance of this revolution on personal, institutional and public levels.

Here, what we should primarily do is to look at the tip of the iceberg. By doing just this, we may understand that the Information Revolution has changed our personal lives, relationships and behaviors completely. Even our willing or unwilling surrender to a lifestyle that we could not even imagine a few years ago is a matter for debate in itself. Whatever our age, education, information and communication technologies literacy may be, we are all experiencing the change in question in different forms. People who will witness the period of 1980–2030 will probably witness the greatest process of change ever experienced in history. No revolution in history penetrated lives this rapidly or was radical enough to change people's bodies and even brain functions. This situation, called "information overload" by scientists, created an unbelievable effect on people.

Today, several studies are being conducted with the aim of investigating the effects of the Information Revolution and the digital world and reaching the right results. One of the most interesting ones among these was conducted at the University of Southern California by Dr. Martin Hilbert[5]. The team that carried out the research calculated the average amount of information stored and sent in the world via letters, computers, books and newspapers using a complex formula. Another study was conducted at the University of California-San Diego by Roger Bohn and James E. Short, and it was found that the human brain is exposed to thirty-four gigabytes of information per day[6]. According to *Harvard Business Review* editor and *The Shallows: What the Internet Is Doing to Our Brains* (author: Nicolas Carr), e-mails appeal to one of the most basic instincts in the human brain, learning by curiosity, and they induce addiction this way. As for nother interesting note by the Google CEO Eric Schmidt at a conference in Tahoe CA,

---

5   Hilbert, M. (2012), How much information is there in the "information society"?. Significance, 9: 8–12. doi:10.1111/j.1740-9713.2012.00584.x.

6   Roger Bohn and James E. Short (2012), Measuring Consumer Information, International Journal of Communication 6, 980–1000.

2010: in the digital world of the 21st century, the information created every two days is equivalent to all the information created so far in the history of the world.

All of these studies and opinions indicate valuable and very interesting situations, but the issue that concerns us is different: in this case, is the individual physically and mentally ready for such an overload, or how does he react to it? As such a large change happens in such a short time, what will be the outcome?

Using some analogies, we may predict how our brains will react to this situation. Let us say that we can run a hundred meters in sixteen seconds. We wake up one morning, and for some reason, we start to run a hundred meters in eight seconds. We may say that this will have a certain effect on our body. Due to the exactly two- double capacity, it will be unavoidable that our body will give up after a point. It is also possible to do this in weight-lifting. Let us say we are working out at a gym, and when our arms that lift twenty kilos start to lift fifty kilos once, the effects of this on our muscles and bones will probably be devastatingly destructive. In short, it is inevitable that the result will be destructive when we put a load on our body and organs in excess of their capacity. Just as in running and weight-lifting, we know that our brain also has a limit or capacity. If we assume that we increase the load of information fifteen-fold, which has been demonstrated by the current case and scientific studies, our brain, which is different to our muscles or bones or other organs, chooses to adapt to this situation rather than giving up. In this adaptation process, it provides different defense methods or reduces some of its functions. For example, as the amount and load of information increases, it assumes a mode that is close to hypnosis, and maybe it reduces the time of focusing and concentration. As confirmed by science, the brain choses the option that is easy and fast for itself. For example, it reaches the conclusion that candies with orange-colored packing are orange flavored, directly and without deep evaluation. Hence, the way our mind works, decision mechanisms, perception, senses, and, to cut a long story short, our mental functions directly linked to our brain, operate differently from how they did before. Considering the point of view from the information and message load we are exposed to, there was not such a noticeable and large difference between the generation thirty years ago and that of one hundred years ago. However, let alone the difference between the current generation and the generation thirty years ago, even the difference between the current generation and the one ten years ago is incredible. In this case, when all fields such as advertising, marketing, education and others that target the human mind are designed and planned based on the old mind, it is out of the question that these fields will be successful and effective in the new order. While this situation and being doomed to failure are so obvious, the reason that changes and adaptations do not take place in these fields is that the decision-making mechanisms and current human resources in these fields are resisting a revolution that will make the power and experience they have obsolete. That is, while the situation has changed and old methods and knowledge bases have become useless, persistent usage of these occurs by people who work in these fields and make decisions. I have bad news for them; change is inevitable. *They will either adapt or disappear.*

For me, the changes in social media and identity definitions are the phenomena that most dramatically illustrate the mind-blowing speed and change in the digital world.

Neuroscientist Susan Greenfield: "Modern technology is changing how our brains work. The human identity, the thought that defines each of us, may be facing an unexpected crisis. This is a crisis that threatens the definitions we have formed in long years regarding who we are, what we do and how we behave."

http://www.dailymail.co.uk/sciencetech/article-565207/Modern-technology-changing-way-brains-work-says-neuroscientist.html#ixzz4Hlt6kvXw

Today, most of us are utilizing the benefits of the digital world and using technology actively. However, we cannot see where we stand in the big picture, how digitization affects our lives, and where we are headed to on a personal or social level. Using information and communication technologies actually makes our lives easier in many ways. However, it would not be right to think that we will adapt to this rapid change by using technological developments or social media effectively.

Of course, the Information Revolution, the current conditions of the digital world, affect the relationship of the individual with life, and therefore, our definitions of identity. Although I am not a sociologist or a psychologist, as a communication researcher, I cannot help but look at the point where our relationships are because of digitization, and I closely follow the transformation we are experiencing in our identities.

Identity is how individuals are defined by themselves or in the eyes of others. That is, a person's identities that are determined by others or the whole of society such as the status they have, and their self-formed or selected identity, are different. These identities may be hidden, covered or obvious. Therefore, one must distinguish individual identity and social identity. The person tries to express individually describe, define and express the identity by which they want to define themselves through their clothing-style, culinary preferences, behaviors, beliefs, musical taste, and in summary, the elements that constitute their lifestyle. Despite this, the individual does not have complete influence or control over the formation of social identity. Some of the impression we get when we meet a person consists of their own intended identity description; however, our perception about their identity is largely shaped by *stereotyping*, clichés and our prejudice filters. Thus, these frames form the perception of that person's social identity, sometimes with very intense prejudice. Issues such as the famous economist who took his notes on the airplane in Arabic, received a complaint and was evacuated from the airplane, or the police complaint about the student who built a clock as a term project because of his ethnic background, are the outcomes of the problem of social identity perception that is shaped by prejudices and frames.

> I experienced a similar situation when I was invited to attend a meeting enti-
> tled "Cultural Amphictyony" in Greece organized by Delphi European Cultural
> Center for the fiftieth anniversary of the establishment of the United Nations
> and make a presentation there. During passport control at the airport, the police
> officer asked me where I was going to and what my purpose of visit was. It might
> be that the Capri pants and linen shirt I was wearing due to the hot weather did
> not fit the academic identity in his head; he examined my documents inten-
> sively, looking up and down at me. By murmuring to himself like "academic,
> hmm…" he sent me off with a "dress like an academic and don't make me make
> an effort" look on his face. Identity is definitely not a concept that is genuine to
> the individual. Institutions and even countries have a two-dimensional identity
> structure that consists of the identity they want to transmit themselves and the
> identity that is attributed to them. Nowadays, there is a third dimension in this
> structure: digital identity. Eric Ericson thought of identity as a form of adapta-
> tion. A person's identity is formed as a sense of subjectivity and it is a personal
> entirety. It has continuity. In psychoanalysis, identity is a discreet structure and
> the conflict among differences (I, you, they…).
> Jean Piaget focuses on socialization. Individuals form their identity by internal-
> izing social phenomena. The most significant of these phenomena is language.
> For example, while sexual identity is formed, the child's nature as a male or
> female endows the child with a role. This means there is both biological and
> cultural difference.

Whether we accept it or not, we have an identity not only in the real world, but also in the virtual world. This is sometimes a simple digital identity that we create on websites, applications and through payments, and it is sometimes a number assigned to us by official institutions. Sometimes, we exist in the virtual world with nicknames that are created without our control or e-mail addresses assigned to us without our choice, through a completely different, fictional identity. While we are living with the idea of an identity that belongs to us in our minds, people who look at our identities in the digital world create a different perception about us in their minds. Then they communicate with us in line with this perception. Situations where virtual and real identities are conflicting – while this is an area of discussion for another field than communication – present a brand new and broad subject of research for science.

I encountered one of the most striking examples of this case in Hamburg a short time ago. I went for a Sunday breakfast to the restaurant at the terrace of Le Meridien, which is one of the most highbrow hotels in the city. While I was having my breakfast, a good-looking lady that I did not know approached me. After greeting each other, she asked me if my name was Okan Tanşu. After I confirmed, she told me she already knew. While I still could not make sense of the situation, after I threw off my first surprise, I asked her how she knew me. The answer was simple. "I follow you on Twitter." I was even more surprised when I learned that she was a long-time follower because of my account which I do not take seriously and where I mostly share sports news. Because the things I wrote that I did not find interesting per se which I casually shared, created a different effect on another person, they even created a sort of admiration. After a bit more conversation, she stated that she was there by coincidence; she was undecided about who I was when she saw me, and she took a photo of me from afar without me knowing. She also shared my photo on Twitter and got my identity confirmed this way. Aside from assessing me as if I were a famous person and that she made me feel that way for a moment, I was puzzled in front of her. In the meantime, she was telling me all this with such a natural attitude that she did not even notice that she was intruding into my personal life and violating my privacy. When I told her that I found the situation strange, she said: "But you are a local celebrity!" My surprise went one step above. I was just a regular academic, but I was a famous person for that woman and for who knows whom else. Because of this frame she put me in due to the digital identity I had created, she thought it was so normal that she traced me like a stalker, and took and shared my photos without my permission. This situation showed me again in a striking way that some definitions have changed in the new world.

This is not a case that is unique to me, of course. Everyone in the virtual world is experiencing this identity chaos in one way or another. It is even the case that some social media users who have gained fame in some way due to their different characteristics or posts are so involved in the atmosphere created in that virtual world that they are complaining when they are not treated like celebrities in real life. There are also those pushing this even further and trying to gain various advantages for themselves via their social media accounts. This misconception is also accompanied by the separation between the new generation that is active in the digital world and the old generation. Thus we face different forms of communication and behavior models that go far beyond what we are used to.

A new business model emerged after the initiation of the concept of virtual world celebrities. We are seeing dozens of examples who imitate individuals who earn millions of dollars annually with a business model that monetizes this situation, and those who are looking for ways to earn easy money just by becoming internet celebrities. On the other hand, we should give them some credit; based on the 2016 numbers of *Forbes,* the annual social media income of 12 million USD by the Kardashian siblings should not be underrated.

How did we come to be here?

We were not actually aware of the winds of change while we were entering the century we are now in. We were excited while talking about portable computers, the internet, invention of mobile phones and their prevalence. However, as interpretations were made regarding macro-level generalization while discussing the changes to be brought about by these technologies, we could not accurately predict their effects. Experts were declaring that an Information Revolution would be experienced. It would be a digital revolution that would make our lives and work easier, and bring people, countries and continents together. It was stated that data and information would flow easily, but what kind of an effect the combination of this with personal computers and mobile phones would create could not be predicted, at least not early in the revolution. Many people and institutions listened to the comments made with ease, as if listening to a science-fiction story. Previously, initiation of the changes and revolutions humankind faced, for example, as in the case of the invention of writing or the printing press, took a long time. Some inventions were not adopted, or not applied in real life. Most people, especially ones who had a significant influence on economic structures with the aim of sustaining the status quo, claimed that the change and transformation of digital telecommunications and communication was a temporary situation, instead of accepting it as a revolution. They took the developments only for new technological benefits that would contribute to their field. For example, not many people predicted changes such as the physiological change imposed on humanity, which would almost get bent vertebral bones due to usage of mobile phones. In summary, we were all caught off guard by this Digital Revolution, we interpreted it incorrectly, and we were not able to foresee the revolution that would influence our daily life to an extent exceeding our expectations.

> In the beginning of the Information Revolution, many successful business people did not notice that the developments constituted a revolution. The owner of a very large retail firm to whom we made recommendations about constructing a website in the early 2000s told us that this was a phase and investments that would be made on a website would be a waste. The firm of this honorable gentleman is now proud that the lion's share of their sales comes from the internet.

The intersection point that transforms humanity

There was an important point in relation to the Information Revolution that was ignored. Of course, throughout history, our lifestyle has constantly changed due to wars, technological developments, commercial relationships and changes in communication. Innovations and inventions were flowing through their own routes, and humankind was digesting these developments in a long process and organizing its life. However, in the late 20th century, an unprecedented intersection was experienced in the flow of historical events. Major developments in the fields of international relations, commerce, communication and technology took place in the same period[7]. When these factors that were powerful enough by themselves to change the direction and future of the history of humanity experienced a great transformation in the same period, the synergy created by this led to an unprecedented revolution. Thus it would be mistaken to attribute the formation of the Information Society we are now living in only to digital developments and advances in the digital world. If there were new dynamics in international relations and developments in communication, it would not be possible to achieve a revolution on this scale.

---

7   The visualised graphic can be seen below.

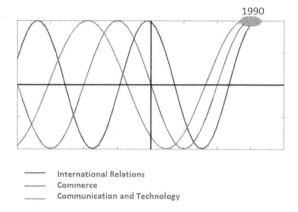

1990

- International Relations
- Commerce
- Communication and Technology

Commerce, economic exchange, investment and financing activities, money markets, entrepreneurship and all connected factors received their share of this change and transformation. Before the Information Revolution took place, such activities would progress in a way that was in harmony with the speed of real life in terms of time. Likewise, telecommunication and communication opportunities were even slower than the speed of real life, and when this was combined with barriers such as blockages in international relations, customs issues and exchange rates, these activities were exceedingly difficult to carry out in comparison to the case today. Tools like phones, fax machines, letters and telex that were used for economic activities were inadequate and insufficient for factors such as money transfers and the basic functions of commercial establishment, imports and exports. As the limited consumption opportunities caused by these issues were combined with the low demand due to people's lifestyles, commercial activities were mostly under the control of a monopoly or a dominant power. Whether a state or an entrepreneur, this monopoly or dominant power would control all trends and lifestyles. Therefore it was highly difficult to find and acquire products not only among firms but also from firms to the end user, or, in technical language, both B2B and B2C. Mutual exclusion of most of the world between parties due to the limitations of communication opportunities and political reasons prevented a change in lifestyle. As a result of this, we would discuss local lives, local consumption and local economies.

If you wanted to buy a car in the previous century, delivery could take months or even years in special cases. This was because demand was high and supply was not high enough to compensate for it, so that, if there were customs walls or similar obstacles, cars would be sold, so to speak, on the black market. If you decide to buy a car today, the delivery time is based on the features you would prefer. If a version with your desired color and features is available in the inventory, good for you. If not, you still need a few months for the version of your preference to be prepared. In other words, it takes months to deliver a car in both periods. The difference is that the delivery time is based on the product in one case, and the consumer in the other case.

The first significant change that triggered the revolution took place with the destruction of the Berlin Wall in the late 1980s, the collapse of the Soviet Union, and therefore the end of the Cold War. This situation led to a transitivity among peoples that were not previously in direct interaction with each other. When one of the most important actors of the Cold War had to leave the competition, the USA became more comfortable in its security/secrecy policies, and provided civil society and commercial businesses with technologies such as the internet and satellites that it had used as tools for intelligence for years. The other superpower of the communist world, China, started a large initiative of technology and commerce with the aim of avoiding the same fate as the Soviet Union.

Hence the economic activity of the 21st century experienced a rapid transition to the digital environment. The wave created by change penetrated to the farthest corners of the world and affected all components of life in a deep and irreversible way. This new revolution was a step that made it impossible to live locally and included people all around the world in communication and interaction. Commercial and economic factors would inevitably be a part of this process. People and organizations that produced the most marginal products and ideas around the world gathered – with speed, which is the most important element in this field – and had the opportunity to establish mutual communication and interaction. Some sectors disappeared, some completely changed, and new business models emerged in the virtual world. Small but specialized firms accessed the chance to do business on a global scale with the help of the Digital Revolution. This development is discussed from a different perspective and in detail in the book David and Goliath by Malcolm Gladwell[8]. Relationships that gathered temporal

---

8   Gladwell, M. (2015). *David and Goliath underdogs, misfits, and the art of battling giants.* New York, NY: Turtleback Books.

speed with e-mail exchanges at first reached a peak through improvements in infrastructures with data and information exchange, photo and video exchange, and finally real-time communication. Various sectors were changed completely by the introduction of mobile phones and devices into the equation.

> *Although Malcolm Gladwell became popular with the book Blink, in my opinion the books Outliers, What the Dog Saw: And Other Adventures are also among those that are worth reading.*

It is a fact that new electronic applications and implementations made our lives easier as they increased transparency and reduced bureaucracy. For example, we no longer have to visit a bank for banking operations. Well, is this the only reason that we placed technology right in the center of our lives?

This question may have various answers; however, the most prominent of the elements that make these more attractive is probably speed. Therefore, we should look at the concept of speed in a broader perspective.

In order to describe the importance of speed in daily life, we may include an example that has a conceptual meaning, but on the other hand makes a problematic comparison. It is stated that the news of the Ottoman Empire conquering Cyprus in the 16th century took about three weeks to reach Istanbul. That is, it took three weeks for an important piece of information to reach the most powerful person in the world at that time. Today, the speed of communication between Cyprus and Istanbul is measured in seconds. If, with an incorrect structure and comparison, we assume that information is power, we might claim that we are much more powerful now than the empire in the 16th century as we acquire information much faster today. While this example is not correctly structured, it provides a good clue about the significance of the speed of technology in our lives today.

In other words, the speed in question is also understood as the speed of the applications brought about by technology. This is correct up to a point. Many of us, with a misconception, use this concept about telecommunication speed only. It is an undeniable reality that applications used in smart devices are increasingly faster in terms of processing power so that, experts have long been stating the idea that hardware cannot reach this mind-blowing speed of software, and to say it in common terms, programmers are flooring the brake pedal. In other words, developments in the world of hardware have difficulty in providing the processes that can already be achieved by products in the software world. There is no doubt that an inequality emerged between the inseparable duo of hardware and software at the point we reached with the Information Revolution. However, while discussing the concepts of the Information Revolution and speed, we must not forget that the speed in question also corresponds to the speed of the flow of money, or information as the financial counterpart of money.

Speed as a concept has another meaning: digital applications make normal life flow faster and have effects on us. For example, the effects of faster processing of an activity that previously took a long time using digital applications on the flow of our lives is a subject for research in itself.

Another dimension of technological speed is the speed of change and innovation it brings. The most important phenomenon revealing this dimension is the void that forms among new technological implementations, our minds that find it difficult to adapt themselves to these regulations, and maybe all elements of the current system.

If we clarify it further: looking at the historical development of humankind, it may be seen that fundamental changes did not take place with the effects of war, engineering, trade or finance, but happened in the framework of acquisition, usage and exchange of information. Before the invention of writing, speaking, forming a common language and using it, which were required for interaction, undeniably allowed humankind to socialize, challenge nature together, and collaborate for hunting and agriculture. Thus the existence of humankind in the world today is a result of the modality of sharing information. Record-keeping by writing and the opportunity to transmit information to new generations that followed it led to another leap in the history of humanity.

The East and the West, two civilizations that evolved and developed in different ways, met as a result of trade over routes such as the Silk Road and wars such as the Crusades, reshaped the information they gathered through exchange in their own ways, and provided new products and experiences. Information filtered through culture led to regional effects with completely different outcomes. Do you not think there is some sort of relationship between spaghetti and noodles? Did the inseparability of spoon and fork in Western culture, and coffee as the part of global culture, not occur with the help of such interactions?

While all these processes were working reasonably, they actually worked towards making technology and information exchange – and telecommunications in a narrower sense – increasingly easier. Throughout the history of humankind, technology has always affected, changed and directed communication.

I will try to describe these three consecutive processes by a figure:

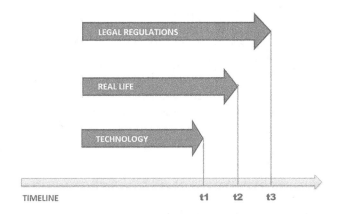

The temporal difference between t1 and t2 in the image shows how fast technology innovated or invented in any geography is reflected in real life. In other words, let us say, it is the time passing from the development of driverless vehicles to their use in daily life. The difference between t2 and t3 is the measurement of the time between usage of these cars in real life and the regulation of the legal situation arising from this usage by the legislations. The important thing here is the length of these time intervals. A long time between t3 and t2 indicates either illegality or lack of technological benefits. Such long times could be tolerated in the past, but now, legislation should have such dynamism that it should be able to work at a speed to regulate all new technological usage and prevent any injustice or problems. The length of this time is also an indicator of the development of a country.

Therefore legal regulations will create more problems as the temporal difference in the relationship of real life and technology grows. Legal reflexes that have become clumsy in suitability for the structure of the industrial society and hard to operate due to bureaucracy cannot keep up with the speed of real life that is shaped by the speed of technology. It is seen that the new lifestyles shaped by the Internet of Things and driverless cars will also face similar issues. Regulatory problems that arise with the usage of technology-based products in real life will become increasingly abundant and reach an unmanageable level. While the information law literature that has developed in the last two decades has shown significant development, it does not possess a capacity to legally respond to new implementations and products that emerge daily. The recent problem that arose with delivery using drones in the USA is a good example of this. The problem was finally solved by bringing a regulation that required all unmanned air vehicles to be registered in order to prevent problems for airplanes in 2015[9]. Likewise, regulations about driverless cars, traffic rules, and, more importantly, insurance regulations, are insufficient for solving the problems that could arise in their current form. Similarly, as there is no regulation about the areas of usage for transportation vehicles such as e-bikes and e-scooters, it was proposed to categorically ban these in certain places in a way that is against the spirit of the 21st century.

According to some views, although technology brings big and significant changes, it will take decades for it to be accepted and popularized. In my opinion, this view was valid up until recently, but now, every innovation that makes life easier and is cheaper than the current options will create a space for itself and rapidly become popularized fast. Attempts were initially made to ban Hyperloop, proposed by the brain of the firm Tesla, Elon Musk, and considered to change transportation from scratch, or in other words, the technology of train carriages that are planned to move in a tube at seven hundred km/h with a magnetic mechanism, in the USA for various reasons, and several problems were speculated about. Despite this, the United Arab Emirates, the Scandinavian countries, the Netherlands and France adopted this technology and have already started to plan its realization. For me, looking at this angle, the concept of speed that we may be discussing in different contexts is a great revolutionary power in accepting and popularizing new technologies.

Today, we can be informed about developments in other parts of the world immediately. However, our failure to adapt to speed, which has direct effects on our lifestyle in different dimensions as mentioned before, deeply influences our private lives, behaviors and relationships. In our time, different ghettos, groups and jobs still continue to emerge within places in the digital world. Romantic relationships are born and bred in the virtual environment. The generation gap is increasingly and irreversibly getting wider. Our values and understanding of morality change. People who know each other are becoming strangers; they cannot communicate, and they get lonelier. Aside from having difficulty in understanding the digital world, we are now also finding it difficult to understand where and in which neighborhood we belong in the real world.

Post-Truth The disappointment of intellectual elites

There are different words corresponding to the conceptual meaning of information in various languages, but especially in English as it is widely used around the world. These include "knowledge" and "information. Therefore, the period

---

9   Joseph Steinberg (December 16, 2015). "Drones in America Must Now Be Registered. Here's What You Need to Know". *Inc.* Retrieved December 16, 2015.

conceptualized by the term "Information Society" actually referred to all elements that are made usable in an analog or digital way by processing data in various forms, becoming the basis for the process of production in society. However, in time, this fundamental approach was replaced by reference to a digital ecosystem where, in addition to production processes, all daily life applications including energy, transportation, communication and telecommunication exist and live with the Information Society. When the information society started to make some noises in the early 1990s, a proud smile appeared on the faces of the intellectual elite who were fetishists of culture and erudition. These sections of society started to have a strong belief that the enlightenment that had been sought for centuries would arrive. It was believed that, with the benefits of the Information Society, society would be enlightened and intellectually developed, science would advance, and universities would be more powerful and become more important in society. While these predictions were partly realized in time, the improvements moved in a direction that was not expected at all. Applications that could be easily consumed by wide audiences that would make their lives easier and appeal to the instincts of humankind such as socialization, exhibition and learning became the main dynamic in the Information Society and digital ecosystem. In this case, highly cultural information sharing or global and fast sharing of information by itself did not make the masses more cultured or knowledgeable. The masses tended towards the things that were easier and more attractive. The photograph of food eaten by a stranger, the video of a place never visited, pictures of an exhibitionist, the last state of someone who was estranged in the past, became more interesting and consumable than the archives opened for access by some of the largest and most prominent libraries in the world. The masses, contrary to the expectations of elite intellectuals, utilized the benefits of the Information Society to the extent of their intellectual levels. Well, of course, what was consumed and desired more became the thing that was dominant and popular. The situation that is called "snowball effect" occurred, and as sub-culture products were consumed, these became abundant. Additionally, after social media such as Facebook and Twitter came into the situation, the digital media did not become a place that eliminated ignorance, but a place that allowed ignorant people to see others like themselves and act more boldly in ignorance. In other words, the intellectual elite thought that they would win the fight against ignorance with the benefits of the information society, but it did not happen. Digital chances were taken by the ignorant, and ignorance started to be presented as a desirable characteristic in a way. By sentences that started "it was in the old times", even the universal values and criteria that had been accepted for centuries started to be debated and insulted. Contrary to expectations, the ignorant became dominant. The case was even that the most obviously incorrect information started to be shared because it was revealed that an audience that would believe it always existed. Society was introduced to the new concept of "post-truth". According to the Oxford English Dictionary, this concept, which was chosen as the word of 2016, is defined as an adjective and means "the case where objective information and facts are less effective than emotions and personal opinions to set the public opinion on a certain subject". This means that, whatever the truth may be, people will not believe in this truth, but trust their own opinions – yet the view that these opinions are shaped by opinion-leaders should not be undermined – and behave accordingly. The audience that previously reached these opinion leaders via a physical environment on limited media have now interacted with them on a global scale, and post-truth has gained a large impact and power.

In summary, although a knowledge based on thousands of years has been opened up to unlimited access and thousands of open-source applications have been provided, this high culture only appealed to a certain audience, but did not contribute to the cultural level of society. As opposed to this, because digital opportunities made communication and telecommunication faster and more prevalent, the uneducated audiences that found people like themselves with ease have become more bigoted, insistent and patronizing about their opinions.

The situation I am trying to describe here, of course, created great discomfort among the intellectual elite. The new habits of this audience were looked down upon and belittled with arrogance and disdain. By the time it was understood that this was not a temporary situation but a permanent one, the panic we experienced in 2017 emerged. Especially during and in the aftermath of the American presidential election, it was seen that this audience belittled by the intellectual elite actually has a considerable influence on the political and international environment. In the Information Society, which was expected to increase their power, the intellectual elite lost the bird already in the hand. In my opinion, this group is mistaken in its reaction towards this situation. Instead of trying to understand the now more dominant majority and its dynamics, they are telling it what it needs to do and trying to impose their concepts and values upon it. Especially in award ceremonies and TV shows in the USA, these disdainful speeches by artists and condemnations of the resulting situation with a headmaster-like attitude create the opposite effect and make this audience more repulsive and unpleasant. The opposite audience is consolidated even more. The intellectual mind is facing a dilemma. Even a great actress like Meryl Streep received responses to her arrogant speech at the 2017 Golden Globes awards ceremony in a way she did not expect.[10]

Today, having high culture and intellectual experience is not appreciated as much. Even its values are not important. There are other concepts which have gained importance. There are millions of people on social media who attack everyone. They carelessly say what comes into their minds even though they would not disrespect them at all if they met in real life. These two audiences could not meet in the past due to various reasons. Neither economic nor social conditions allowed it, but the situation has changed now. People from all groups are together on social media platforms. In this case, there is an emergence of an audience who can refer to a group that they could previously not spill out their hatred for and speak to in a way that they want. Such an environment of "freedom" was born for the first time. The intellectual elite who are not used to this naturally feel great discomfort about this situation. Denying social media, ignoring it or trying to stay out of it may be one method or defense mechanism, but it is obvious that it will not change the truth, and it is only running from the truth. If the intellectual elite cannot decide on what kind of a place and a role it will set for itself in the new world intellectual ecosystem and follow the right path, it is the end for them. We may argue that they will certainly disappear in at most thirty years. For this, firstly the education system, educators, educational institutions and the content of education would have to change and adapt to the new order. I think that starting this with universities rather than primary schools would be a good step to make this process faster.

A new discrimination: Digicrimination

With the magnificent waves created by the change in question, we started to be divided amongst ourselves knowingly or unknowingly, especially between people who use technology and those who do not. The interesting thing is that we attribute negative adjectives to both groups. While people who use technology less are deemed to be modern, we call those who frequently utilize these opportunities technology addicts. People who always use technology in their lives may sometimes be accused of indifference about subjects such as love of nature, friendship or environmental awareness. You will remember how much this group

---

10 Gonzalez, S. (2017, January 15). Meryl Streep attacks Trump in Golden Globes acceptance speech. Retrieved in 2017, from http://edition.cnn.com/2017/01/08/entertainment/meryl-streep-golden-globes-speech/index.html.

is sometimes discriminated against with an image that occasionally goes viral on social media. In this image, a notice attached to the window of a restaurant that does not provide Wi-Fi for its customers gets attention. It reads: "We do not provide Wi-Fi because we want you to talk to each other." While this `not' on the window of the restaurant has a humorous tone, does it not use a language that excludes technology users? Concepts like (Digital Detox) that refers to quitting using digital devices and (Digital Nomad) that refers to people who continue their jobs in different parts of the world with the help of digital connection, have already found a place in the Turkish language.

> The relationship between the digital world and language is discussed by several researchers and the way the language used and vocabulary are affected and changed in the digital age is revealed. Academics such as Ann Curzon, Ben Zimmermann and David Crystal are busy with this issue. I am curious about another thing. Did the speed of the digital world in question also affect our speed of speech? Are we speaking at a faster pace or is it still the same?
> At an entirely unscientific guess, if we assume people use their visual sense more in the digital world and people who use their visual sense more intensely speak at a faster pace, I think the pace of the speech of future humans will increase.

In summary, it would not be wrong to argue that we have been divided into those who gained a place in new digital ghettos and those who did not, in this new world created by the Information Revolution, and into those who understand the new language and new way of communication that emerged and those who do not Thus, the book in your hand refers to this division in question, a new way of discrimination that I call Digicrimination.

In this book, while I will try to describe the sectors affected by Digicrimination such as education, marketing and entrepreneurship, I will also try to look at the impact on relationships, addictions and humane behaviors. Digicrimination is a concept which I created using the words Digital and Discrimination. Differing from Digital Divide, which can be mostly defined as an economic and social inequality in access to information and communication technologies (ICT), Digicrimination is the discrimination phenomenon faced by some members of society because they are not able to understand, use or access information and communication technologies (ICT) and all the applications created by those technologies[11.] I

---

11 U.S. Department of Commerce, National Telecommunications and Information Administration (NTIA). (1995). *Falling through the net: A survey of the have nots in rural and urban America*. Retrieved from, http://www.ntia.doc.gov/ntiahome/fallingthru.html.

will start with new phenomena, concepts and technological structures caused by the Digital Revolution, and while I have no intention to become a futurist, I will talk about the new revolution awaiting us in the future in the last part of the book. I must also say that the Digital Revolution is so fast and so mind-blowing that I believe it would be wrong to make predictions going further than today. The actual purpose here is to guide those readers who have difficulty in seeing and perceiving the entirety of the current situation, and want to understand the new dynamics. My priority is to present the changes in progress that have already been created by the Digital Revolution and how these changes will affect us in the next few years.

So who is taking part in this discrimination? Precisely the new life and lifestyles created by the digital world. This new type of living imposes a barrier between people who use digital opportunities and those who do not, and favors those who do. This favoring is not only limited to benefits for people who use digital opportunities to the furthest extent, but also implies various difficulties for those who do not. This is a new type of discrimination; it is the digitized form of discrimination that has adapted to the Age of Information. A Digital Discrimination.

In order to make this narrative as simple as possible, we should first start with new concepts brought into being by the Digital Revolution: a new IQ model, ICTIQ (Information and Communication Technology IQ), CBD (Chip Based Device) which refers to the chip-based devices that are part of our daily lives, Screen Addiction and Digital Schizophrenia which entered our lives with computers and smartphones, the Internet of Things, and Digital Discrimination. It is actually possible to include various concepts in addition to these that grew up within the Digital Revolution. However, I chose these particular concepts as they are the ones that form the core of the radical transformation of humanity and trigger the debate regarding Digicrimination.

New concepts or those that are renewed with the Digital Revolution create new tendencies, business models and behaviors in the areas they took under their influence. Individual, economic and international relationships are reshaped. Digicrimination, by discussing these relationships from another perspective over the new communication model, aims to make some recommendations for those who want to draw up a road map. If you are lost because of the strong waves created by the Digital Revolution or you find it difficult to catch the right stream although you have determined a route, Digicrimination may help you navigate.

Section 2. Discovering new concepts

Whenever I am invited to a TV or radio show to share my views, my friends, acquaintances and colleagues share similar complaints: "You spoke very well, told it clearly, but we did not understand much of what you were talking about." In the past, I would think that this is about my professional deformation. After all, whether they are in natural sciences or social sciences, the technical language used by academics is usually found complicated and hard to understand by audiences that are not familiar with the field. The result I reached by myself over time indicated another reason. I was actually trying to keep the language I use concise, but it was not easy for everyone to understand the new concepts and definitions brought into being by the digital world. The terms I used either did not have the same sense for the audience in front of me, or their conceptual definitions were not the same for everyone. In some cases, these concepts would not have been sufficiently studied. Apparently, we were finding it difficult to surpass the definitions and concepts placed in our minds by the industrial society and communicate through a newly-emerging language.

Sometimes definitions, descriptions and names established for new innovations became obsolete. At other times, I was talking about so many innovations one after another that it was becoming hard to adopt and understand the definitions that came with these. It was possible that even audiences that followed the digital world closely might be uninformed about newly emerging definitions. This situation made me face the necessity of establishing a new explanation about the new concepts imposed by the digital world and create a new common language. As a set of innovations started to enter our lives, I could not help but provide the definitions that I thought would describe these innovations in the best way. I hope that, as these concepts that are the subjects of Digicrimination become prevalent, solutions will be created at least for conceptual problems and communication issues imposed on us by the digital world.

I believe that the new world created by the Digital Revolution is like a new country for many of us. If we want to know about the streets, people and culture of this strange country, we need to learn at least a few words of the language of the country. Therefore, before going on to the sectors or behaviors changed by the Digital Revolution, I wanted to start by defining new concepts. After all, I believe that these concepts will help us express ourselves better to those who are living in this new country we are visiting, communicate better with them, and participate more in cultural and social activities.

In addition to those working in the most technical fields of the informatics sector, we are already encountering the new concepts of the digital world mentioned by professionals working in fields such as communication, sociology or psychology in newspapers, meetings and conversations. However, some you will see in this book are concepts that I discovered, personally defined and emphasized as a result of my long academic studies in the subjects of communication and digitization, like Digicrimination, which is the title of the book. This definition refers to a new type of discrimination imposed on individuals who are excluded from new business models or types of relationships because they could not keep up with the change brought by digitization. We may use this division for groups that are excluded, for example, from the "Digital Ghettos" that I observed and named through my work. As you might expect, I am using the concept of Digital Ghetto to describe the ghettos formed by people in the digital world who gather at sometimes professional, sometimes social common points. I actually started to realize the phenomenon of Digicrimination during a vacation in the early 2000s. I learned that there was heavy construction work near the hotel I was planning to stay at from comments on the internet, and then I cancelled my booking at the last minute and went to another hotel. When I went on my vacation and passed by the hotel in question by coincidence, I witnessed the predicament of the customers of the hotel, and noticed the advantage provided to me by accessing this small but significant piece of information. Both the customers of that hotel and I had worked a whole year for this vacation. However, they were discriminated against, and they did not even know about it. While this discrimination differed from the traditional types of discrimination such as religious or ethnic discrimination, it was still discrimination.

TripAdvisor may be the largest platform that includes opinions and criticisms of consumers on their travels, and allows them to share these. The information on this platform has such a large scope that it is now possible to access consumers' views about the smallest restaurant in the middle of nowhere. Moreover, with scientific analysis, it is possible to access information about the travel habits of millions of people, which is highly crucial for the tourism sector. This situation could not even be imagined, not long, but only twenty years ago.

We will actually witness the development of concepts that are in the current agenda in the Digital Revolution through the years. New ones will even appear in no time, and some of the applications that we think of as "how did we live without them?" will disappear. After all, the Digital Revolution is increasingly gaining speed and advancing every day. Here, without futuristic speculation, I would like to emphasize some high-priority concepts that are influencing our lives or those that we expect to be influencing our lives in a short time.

The new concept that evaluates digital usage instead of intelligence: ICTIQ (Information and Communication Technology IQ)

IQ (Intelligence Quotient) is value provided by tests applied with the purpose of measuring our intelligence. The concept of IQ emerges as a result of the need of the people in the industrial society created by the Industrial Revolution to understand and use recently-developed technology and innovations. In this period, in the light of the hypothesis that an intelligent person would be superior and have greater advantages over others in their personal and professional life, IQ measurements started. It was expected that those with higher IQ values than others would find better job positions and establish happier relationships. However, towards the ends of the industrial age, it was observed that high IQ is not sufficient for correct efficiency. In other words, high efficiency and high IQ were not proportionate. After this, various measurements such as Emotional Quotient and Curiosity Quotient were proposed. These measurements even came to be used in some cases of employment and some educational institutions to an extent that would lead to discrimination.

When we arrived at the end of 1990, ICT (Information and Communication Technology) usage became an important factor in increasing efficiency. People needed to gain new skills and improve themselves to use these technologies effectively. Therefore, the concept of ICT or informatics literacy came into our lives. However, learning to use any technological application would not be sufficient by itself. It was revealed in time that ICT literacy should be combined with thinking skills and creating business from an ICT perspective in order to increase efficiency, and later, the concept of ICTIQ that I proposed was born out of this process. Accordingly, only those individuals who show the ability to combine two paradigms came to be defined with high ICTIQ.

Therefore I must indicate that the ICTIQ concept that we will use in the following sections of the book is one that is independent from IQ. While IQ is required for perfect usage and internalization of ICT, ICTIQ does not place digital usage into the mental atlas. ICTIQ is a value that will be used to measure our level of communicating with digital devices and information technologies. In fact, there is no standardized scale for this material yet. Even so, it is clear that we need to have ICTIQ to achieve success in the new ecosystem we are living in.

In rough terms, IQ is used to express the intellectual intelligence quotient and mental skills. EQ (Emotional Quotient) is a measurement unit regarding the capacity of a person to understand and manage their emotions towards themselves or others, while CQ (Curiosity Quotient) is used to measure the level of curiosity and intellectual hunger. As it is a rare occurrence that any person has high values in all three of these measurements, questions arise as to what kind of score is necessary for which job and what kind of education may be provided towards it. Now we have the new measurement method of Q. I think the main issue starts now, especially in the field of education.

The new face of social intelligence

Before looking in detail at how the concept of ICTIQ affects some certain fields of work transformed by the Digital Revolution, we may make the definition clearer by a few small examples.

Let us assume two different cases. In the first one, there is a person who works with high technology – for example, a dentist who uses high technology devices such as an x-ray machine or a laser while performing their profession. The dentist in question is a person who is not very familiar with technology. On the other hand, let us think about the scenario that this dentist cannot solve the problem when they experience an issue with their mobile phone or TV remote. Is this dentist's failure to solve this problem based on the age group or generation they belong to? Or is there another factor that is effective? The answer to this question is actually hidden in the name of this book.

In the second case, let us discuss a conversation between a grandmother and her grandson. Let us assume the grandson tells his grandmother: "I met a very beautiful girl today and I think I may be in love." The grandmother: "How nice! How is she? Is she blonde? Is she tall? What is the color of her eyes?"

After this, it is possible that the grandson will answer his grandmother like this: "I don't know, grandmother. I haven't seen her yet. We met at a chat room on the internet."

It must be very difficult for the grandmother to understand such a situation. As we know that internet usage habits are not related to what generation we belong to, we may also include others in this example. These two examples actually demonstrate tous that usage of information technologies is so important regardless of age or profession. In order to be able to do this, we need to be on a certain ICTIQ level.

What I have in mind: Are there any implicit and genuine cultures, accepted codes, jargon, rules, manners in instant messaging groups, forums and social media any more? If the answer is "yes", then how are these cultures, codes or similar limitations and lines determined? For example, how are Instagram and Twitter different in this matter, and where do they converge?

Digital life is not limited to the virtual world: CBD

Many people think that information and communication technologies consist only of computers and the internet. However, I think this proposition is incorrect. Mobile technologies and especially mobile phones are an important part of today's information technologies. The concept of mobility has a highly significant place in the process of communication; however, its aspects such as online games, listening to excerpts from new songs and conversation are at least as revolutionary as mobility itself. Today, a mobile phone is an indispensable personal usage device, rather than an accessory like a watch. With the phenomenon of convergence, while there may be various applications including radio, TV, video features, GPS (Global Positioning System) and other in mobile phones, would it be realistic to say all these tools do not change our lifestyle?

On the other hand, the fact that we are now accessing the internet from everywhere is an important part of the Digital Revolution. Fast access to the internet and all kinds of information creates an important difference in our quality of life. However, it would not be right to mention only the virtual world, the internet or games we access via mobile phones and computers while talking about the concept of digital life. We are actually taking part in digital life in various activities of ours in real life by using CBDs (Chip Based Devices).

After the Information Revolution, some companies designed and produced specialized devices for various sectors. Devices that provide the means for instant communication for units that need to be in contact with each other quickly found their place in the market, especially in places that rely on speed such as restaurants and cafes. CBDs, naturally, not only created a new style in the field in question, but virtually redefined the field. At first the technological foundations were not suitable for these devices, but when it became suitable in time, it became inevitable to use these devices. Examples of CBDs include offline devices that utilize SIM cards or wireless connections such as POS machines. Measurement devices, architecture/drawing/engineering devices, screens that show our number in banks, screens in cars, navigation devices and many others may be defined as CBD.

> We are actually taking part in digital life in various activities of ours in real life by using CBDs, or chip based devices.

Besides, none of these devices are conventionally related to the machine we call a computer. These are devices that were designed to make life and usage easier. RF (Radio Frequency) loyalty cards are also a good example of CBDs. The high amounts of data (Big Data) collected through these cards have become a significant value for companies. Firms can use these data and organize their sales and marketing activities in the light of these by examining consumer behavior down to the smallest detail.

Ideas sharpened in the virtual worlds: Digital Ghetto

We are all familiar with the definition of ghetto. Residential areas where a certain minority lives in a city are called ghettos. Indeed, the ghetto is a structure that has been around since the Middle Ages. It is a structure that formed as a result of feudal lords and the people living in separate places in earlier times. In the structure of feudalism, serfs and villagers established their own living spaces by saying "this is our area" by their own will or as a result of landowners' impositions. This class difference did not disappear in the industrial societies that emerged after the Industrial Revolution, but grew. The feudal structure then evolved into the division of employee-employer. If you visited various cities in Europe, you might have encountered signs that read "this used to be a Jewish neighborhood" and notices that explain the history of the area regarding these signs. For one reason or another, in agricultural society after permanent settlement and especially in industrial society with urbanization, it became a perfectly natural case that people coming from similar classes, religions and ethnic backgrounds gathered in one neighborhood. In this context, the significance of a ghetto is that it is an area where similar people live together. Ghettos, formed by people gathered together sometimes for religious and sometimes for racial reasons, would usually make contact with the outer world in a limited manner for the purpose of shopping. Marriages and social relationships would be formed in this closed system. Is it not still like this in many places?

Let us say we are in a Portuguese neighborhood in Germany, namely a ghetto. There is a separate culture in this ghetto. When someone or some effect comes from outside, this effect is evaluated in that neighborhood based on the dynamics of the ghetto. These ghettos have people who are dominant that we define as the opinion leaders of the ghetto. These people need not necessarily have a religious, political or social identity. They have an influence of the dwellers in the ghetto through their privileged, prioritized statuses that are defined in some context.

Ghettos in the virtual world

Today, the same structure is also seen in the digital world. Various ghettos started to be formed in the virtual world, on social media, forums, instant messaging applications or similar digital communication platforms. I call these ghettos "Digital Ghettos". The difference between Digital Ghettos and conventional ghettos is that the digital ones are places where similar people from different geographies gather. This means they do not have to be from the same ethnicity, religion or country. A group of people who like Iron Maiden and do not listen to Metallica may very well constitute a ghetto in the virtual environment. We may also talk about Digital Ghettos formed by the fans of a sports team. Before social media was so powerful, these establishments were created via forums. Then people started to form their own groups on social media. Even further than this, own digital platforms, applications and communication software of these groups started to appear. These applications that gather only people from a certain ethnicity, religion or similar sub-social group, are a form of discrimination in real life transferred to the digital world in some way. However, the Digital Discrimination in our book discusses another issue.

In fact, just like in real ghettos, there is a dominant sense of being a group in Digital Ghettos too. There are also opinion leaders here. There is a relationship with the outer world to some extent. When outsiders try to join the group, they are not easily accepted and they face resistance. Personal psychology of ghetto members is also effective here. Especially if the person who is coming from outside is talking about concepts that are frowned upon by the group, they find it difficult to gain acceptance as a different voice and they are excluded.

Suppose you are going to buy a product on the internet. Do you not go further than checking the product information, read the comments of previous purchasers and become affected? While choosing between similar products, if you are making your purchase under the influence of comments even though you are not certain of their accuracy, this means you are under the influence of that opinion leader. If a person who shares thousands of comments on a product profiled on Amazon is not an opinion leader, what is he?

On the other hand, as these people living in a Digital Ghetto follow only the posts by the groups that they feel they belong to when they visit the virtual world, they may stay uninformed about the opinions of people outside these groups. They get sharpened through their opinions only, and even worse, they may say "this means my opinion is the best" by assuming the outer world shares the same opinions.

The falsest and most illogical opinion may turn into reality and become true/fact. If the person is sharing an opinion that disagrees with the opinions asserted in the digital ghetto, they cannot share it, or they hide this opinion. People who are afraid of the type of virtual verbal abuse that is called cyber- bullying do not want to face the reaction that will come from the ghetto. These environments constantly produce common friends or enemies. The reality in the world may easily be missed.

Moreover, people in Digital Ghettos started to assume more than one identity. We may force our imagination and provide the following example: it is very hard for a person on the digital communication platforms of the St. Pauli football team in Hamburg, which has a left-wing fan base, to come out and say, "long live capitalism!" This message may be perceived as betrayal of the cause in the Digital Ghetto that the person is in. Using this example, we may say that opinions in Digital Ghettos are constantly sharpened due to being in communication in an environment that is always enclosed. Even though the ghetto in question is hypothetical, we may encounter several similar oxymoronic situations in Digital Ghettos.

The most important difference of Digital Ghettos from the ghettos in real life is that they face the strength of the memory of the internet. In fact, if we express it by the popular saying: the internet never forgets. During any discussion, a post you shared five years ago may be revealed and what you said in the past may be used against you. Additionally, the concept of cyber-bullying is also increasingly globalized by the prevalence of Digital Ghettos.

The first places where Digital Ghettos gathered were chat rooms, which were very popular in the late 1990s. Then mail lists came up, which were followed in tu by forums, social media groups and finally today's highly popular instant messaging groups. These applications that have their own dynamics have experienced many evolutions and changes over a period of twenty years. Let us wait and see the next place where Digital Ghettos will be established. It is certain that we need a highly interesting application to attract people and become appealing.

Oh my God! Am I going mad? : Digital Schizophrenia

While describing the concept of Digital Ghetto, we had the chance to mention the illusions experienced by people who are active in these groups. However, the effects of the Digital Revolution on human psychology are in fact much deeper than we imagine. A friend of mine is a hardcore computer gamer. Recently, he took an interest in car racing games among these groups. In the game he was playing, he designed a car that was an exact replica of the car he had in the real world. He even follows the routes that he uses in real life in some stages of the game. My friend had a major accident while he was going back home with his car. The car had extensive damage after he failed to take a corner in a curve. When I visited him to share my good wishes, I asked about how the accident happened. The response shocked me. My friend responded: "I couldn't pass the curve I cornered every day, though I never had a problem there in the game." I could not hide my surprise and said: "What you are experiencing is a certain case of Digital Schizophrenia! You were cornering there with your car in the computer game, not in real life…"

Name dot last initial @ company dot com!

We were actually introduced to the concept of Digital Schizophrenia in the late 1990s when we got our first e-mail accounts. The IT employees in the workplace where we were working did not only create an e-mail account for us, but they also asked, "What do you want your name to be?" After point, we learned that IT employees could read what we wrote in our e-mail accounts over the servers used by the system and developed anxiety. However, thinking that we might protect our privacy when the servers were far away, we opened up new accounts outside the workplace by using portals such as Hotmail. We saw that we were able to use even our favorite football player's or actress's name when creating these accounts. We registered more than one e-mail address and used these accounts for different things. In this way, we created multiple identities for ourselves.

When we were experiencing different identities in e-mail correspondences, we started to use a different language in the chat windows we opened on our workplace computers. Today, we have different identities on many social media platforms and virtual environments from Facebook to Twitter. The same person may post one comment on Facebook and a completely different one on Twitter. They may be tweeting on Twitter in a way to please or maybe entertain their followers, but sharing posts in a different framework for a completely different environment and set of friends on Facebook.

Besides all these developments, people have now started to create their own avatars for games or platforms that are called Virtual Reality. People there have created unique characters for themselves. All these characters and identities started to create behavioral disorders in people. In summary, I call this identity crisis that people experience as Digital Schizophrenia.

The new dimension of identity confusion

The concept of identity, of course, is not unique to the individual. The identity we find suitable for ourselves may differ from the identity assigned to us by society. That is, personal and social identities should be examined separately. Institutions and countries are also included in this two-dimensional definition of identity. However, with digital identity, there is now a third dimension to this definition. In this case, this situation frequently leads individuals, institutions and countries to face an interesting conflict.

If we consider the issue of identity confusion on an individual level, the conflict a person experiences between their real and virtual identity leads to Digital Schizophrenia. Individuals who cannot assume the identity they want in real life due to various reasons such as motivation to suppress social pressure, shame, fear or similar emotions find a free area for themselves in the digital world. With the chance created by the internet, especially in the 1990s, to become and stay anonymous, people have gained the chance to create the identities they envied in real life in the digital world. Therefore, they gained the opportunity to experience any identity they desired without any pressure. While opportunities for anonymity in the virtual environment diminished over time, they did not disappear. On the other hand, the number of people who cherished this freedom with their digital identities increased instead of decreasing.

Individuals started to experience psychological traumas because of the different identities they established. Individuals who considered themselves closer to their identity in the virtual environment than that in the real world, are experiencing great difficulty in returning to their real identity. I tie this trauma to the phenomenon of Digital Schizophrenia. This issue experienced by individuals is now being experienced by institutions, too. We are meeting a person or an institution at first via their virtual identity, develop an opinion about them and produce a definition. Then, when we face the reality, we may sometimes encounter considerable differences. While there are several academic studies being conducted about Digital Schizophrenia and its outcomes, it is crucial to predict how it will penetrate the DNA of society, calculate its results and most importantly, estimate its long-term effects.

I was surprised at first when I read an article on the contagious nature of the mental state on social media. My surprise became even greater when I met an entrepreneur who analyzes words used on social media and estimates changes in gold and silver exchanges later. In fact, it is a field that needs to be taken seriously and studied extensively as social media is used to analyze the economic, political and social flow in real life.

[Experimental evidence of massive-scale emotional contagion through social networks, Adam D. I. Kramer, Jamie E. Guillory, and Jeffrey T. Hancock, Author Affiliations Edited by Susan T. Fiske, Princeton University, Princeton, NJ, and approved March 25, 2014] [12]

What if I am missing something? : Screen Addiction

While we are experiencing Digital Schizophrenia due to multiple identities created in the virtual world, we are also observing effects of the posts shared on social media on our behaviors. One should not think that we are increasingly being driven mad by these posts by considering the examples I provided for Digital Schizophrenia. Studies show that posts shared on social media sometimes have positive effects, too.

People's desire to present their lives to each other as colorful and fun leads them to share posts that say, "Look, how happy I am!" Thus, people are trying to photograph the moments they seem happy, views of the vacation they took and food they ate and share these on social media as much as possible. However unhealthy this might seem, it has a positive side, too. Studies show that human nature is affected by the aspects of the posts shared. This means when people constantly see happy photos and read happy posts, their sense of happiness increases.

This case which has exploded on social media has led people to start to stalk others with curiosity. People who carried this stalking further are exposed to the problem that we call Screen Addiction.[13]

---

12 Adam D. I. Kramer, Jamie E. Guillory, and Jeffrey T. Hancock (2014) Experimental evidence of massive-scale emotional contagion through social networks, PNAS, Vol 111 No 24, Edited by Susan T. Fiske, Princeton University, Princeton, NJ, and approved March 25, 2014.

13 Andrew K.; Murayama, Kou; DeHaan, Cody R.; Gladwell, Valerie (July 2013). "Motivational, emotional, and behavioral correlates of fear of missing out". *Computers in Human Behavior*. **29**: 1841–1848.

> The actual motivation behind Screen Addiction is the sense of "what am I missing when I am not online", Experts describe this tendency as Fear of Missing Out (FOMO).

Some people are stuck looking at their smartphones with the purpose of not missing what is happening on social media or in the virtual world, or sometimes they are stuck in front of the computer screen as they cannot help but play games and race others …

In midnight movie screening sessions which I deeply enjoy as they are quiet , I watch people who get bored with some parts of the movie and look at their phones with interest. I am sure you have seen it many times, too. Some do it because of Screen Addiction, while other do it due to the Digital Schizophrenia they have developed with the anxiety of being in the movie theater and the virtual world at the same time. Indeed, what might be the thing at that hour of the night that would feel more interesting than the movie in the theater and direct attention towards the smartphone?

A person who works in the film industry and wants to understand if the movie will work may actually sit at the back of the theatre, watch the people and obtain very valuable information. It would be really easy to look at the phone lights going on and off in the theatre and monitor the times where the pace of the movie is lost or attention is diverted from the movie. All jokes aside, social media usage during sports matches that we watch with joy, which usually increases adrenalin, is so high that it is really difficult to understand whether the viewers are watching the match or sharing posts on social media at the time.

People cannot lift their heads from their smartphones even at dinners they go to with their friends, and cannot help but follow social media. They want to constantly check social media and see what is happening when they are sitting at home reading a book or watching TV. This is why people take out their phones right at the moment when the airplane touches down at the airport.

Section 3. Digital traces in every aspect of life

Not technological, but structural transformation in sectors

The concepts that play a leading role in Digicrimination such as ICTIQ, CBDs, Digital Schizophrenia, Screen Addiction and the Internet of Things which I have tried to describe using current examples affect all aspects of life in different ways. While fields such as education and government/governance were restructured in the last two decades in consideration of changes imposed by the Digital Revolution, these changes did not go beyond the use of new technologies. Attempts were made to achieve the transition that was required by the Digital Revolution by basing it on the usual industrial models instead of changing the current infrastructure. However, let alone over the next few years, it is clear that the current structure is insufficient even today.

It seems inevitable that priority sectors that affect our lives such as education, human resources/employment, entertainment, marketing, security and government/governance should internalize the new critical concepts of the Digital Revolution, and go into a model change that is not only technological, but also structural. Moreover, in addition to sectoral fields' ways of functioning, our individual and corporate relationships that are affected by these fields are also being transformed, and most of us are not even aware of this transformation.

It is also important to discuss the effects of concepts such as ICTIQ, CBD, Digital Schizophrenia and Screen Addiction based on critical and priority sectors that are at the center of change. I would like to start this with talking about the structural changes necessitated in these sectors by the Digital Revolution, their historical development and the current positions that took in response to the changes. My primary intention is to discuss the type of transformation experienced by the *current* sectors and fields that have an important place in societal dynamics. We will then look at *new* fields that have emerged. This way, we may observe the big picture and provide recommendations towards the adaptation of the sectors in question to the Digital Revolution.

The pain of transitioning into the Information Society model in education

Education's content and way of presentation have been passed down from generation to generation within the scope of needs since the dawn of humanity. Humankind shaped and developed education in compliance with nature using its basic instincts and passed its information for basic needs such as eating and hunting down to new generations. As the living conditions of humanity improved, philosophical thought also emerged, and there arose a question of transferring significant information regarding beliefs. This transference happened through education based on esoteric information at first. Empirically-obtained information was passed down to future generations.

> Yuval Noah Harari's book Sapiens, which just came out recently and lit the way to understand history with clear and concise language, is a work that needs to be read, just like Guns, Germs, and Steel. Another work by Harari, Homo Deus, also has highly significant projections about the future.[14]

In Ancient Greece, which is accepted as the basis of Western civilization, the idea of including mathematical and philosophical content in education emerged with structures like the School of Aristotle. In fact, Zen monks and similar groups in the East were transferring information such as self-discipline to their disciples much earlier than the West by certain methods of education. There was a concept of education that was close to the definition that we know in the Middle East and Ancient Egypt in fields such as astrology and astronomy. In the Middle Ages, a dark age started for the West as science was considered as sin, and continued with the activities of the Inquisition. The concept of education continued to be defined within the framework of religion up to the Renaissance and Enlightenment. In the same period in the East, scholars such as Avicenna, Al-Biruni, Al-Khazini and Al-Djazari, who were far ahead of their times, worked on scientific facts that the West reached hundreds of years later, but they could not arouse the necessary interest and effect. While there were educational institutions such as madrasas that provided religious and esoteric education in the East, education in its basic form was viewed in a military sense and priority was given to achieving conquests in order to gain land. The way of education as we know it today had secondary importance and it was not compulsory.

Later on, after the arrival of the Age of Enlightenment, planning education started to be a topic, especially in countries like France. Efforts were made to define the ideal school. Nevertheless, the real importance of literacy was understood though Enlightenment and modernization.

---

14 Harari, Y. N. (2015). *Sapiens: a brief history of humankind.* New York: Harper. Harari, Y. N. (2016). *Homo deus: a history of tomorrow.* Toronto, Ontario: Signal.

Coalition of media and education

New urban life, the birth of the class of bourgeoisie and the development of communication technologies gave rise to a new structure: the media. Development of the media took its place in history as an important dynamic in the field of education with the industrial society. The media, which reached masses through printed materials such as newspapers at first, were actually being used as a tool for a class to express itself in addition to being a tool to distribute the news. This class, consisting of employers or land-owners, had to provide something for the working class to keep them working and producing. Therefore concepts like music, entertainment, and stories through the media came into our lives. Popular culture created an artificial comfort for the workers who were working in harsh conditions, or, in other words, it assumed the role of a social valve and was named as the fourth estate in addition to the legislative, judiciary and executive estates.

Following this structure that emerged with the dynamics of the industrial society and for some time before WWI, there was La Belle Époque (Beautiful Era, 1880–1914). In this period of time which started in France and was defined as a period of abundance and optimism for the class of bourgeoisie who utilized the benefits of industrialization, both education and media experienced a period of change. True or false, a large amount of information was provided to the public and this manipulated information was accepted as true by the masses without question.

What is the first example of media manipulation in the history? The ruler of Egypt who was defeated by the Hittites in the Battle of Kadesh had an inscription that told the opposite engraved on a wall of one of the pyramids. This way, the Pharaoh led the public to believe for a long time that the battle ended in a tie.

On the other hand, civil and secular schools started to be built in cities for the children of the bourgeoisie. Especially in Western societies, children of the working people also gained the opportunity to go to schools in cities and guarantee their future within the capitalist order of industrial society. However, in addition to this, people came to be receiving a part of their education about life from the media and newspapers, which were among the most effective tools of the period. When a new sense, voice, came into the media, that is, when radio became prevalent, there was a significant evolution regarding education. People learned the way to behave and manners from radio theater and educational programs, and started to imitate what they learned. It was important for the people of the period to speak in the way they heard on the radio and use the same language as those they listened to on the radio.

Accents that were spoken in cities which were the pioneers of economic and social change became prevalent as the desirable language, as in the prevalence of Istanbul Turkish in Turkey. It became standard to own a radio device, and access to the news started to occur through the radio in addition to newspapers. Before this period, people received a part of their education from school, and the rest from their friends and close family. While newspapers became commonplace much earlier, the media started to gain such a significant role in education for the first time.

As radio broadcasts were under the monopoly of the state in the industrial society, information provided by the state, just as in the first periods of the media, was internalized by acceptance of it as true. The authoritarian Salazar regime that was in power between the years 1932 and 1968 in Portugal is a good example of this. The Salazar regime took control of the public with the "football, fiesta and fado" manipulation that it achieved over the media, and sustained the dictatorship for long years. People were learning about life from a single source and completing their education this way, and they were creating a unique social culture for themselves through this manipulation. The peak of this situation was achieved when television became a part of daily life. TV, which had a much stronger appeal to the senses and entered homes in the black and white format at first and in color later, had a significant effect on education. Children learned to shape their behaviors from cartoons and TV shows, in addition to their families. While organizations like the BBC included educational shows such *Sesame Street*, television changed social behavior uncontrollably. It was used to a great extent for social engineering. While there was no equality of education in terms of school, everyone who had a TV set was able to reach relative equality by receiving information through this device.[15]

While television's emergence in the political history and its increased effects on masses are thought to have started in the 1960s, it is accepted that the real milestone in this matter was the failed coup attempt in Spain in 1981 and the speech in the following process by King Carlos that was broadcast on television.

When the universal concept of school changes

Until the Digital Revolution affected our lives, the school and education norms determined by the West were universalized and accepted from Korea to America. The Digital Revolution changed not only our social behavior but also the concept of education; its effects are still ongoing. While accessing information and the

---

15 Madrid, B.C. (1981, February 23). King orders army to crash coup. Retreived in 2017, from; https://www.theguardian.com/world/1981/feb/spain.fromthearchive.

news has become faster and every individual has come to a point to able to provide the news through social media, providers and recipients of information have also changed. Television is still ahead of other communication devices; however, the new generation that was born into the Information Revolution has the skills to simultaneously follow multiple media including TV. They are now improving the education they have received by utilizing all mass communication sources.

The new generation, who gained the skills of multi-screen monitoring with ICTIQ capabilities, has the ability to simultaneously post a tweet and provide information while watching any activity or news. This generation is able to follow affairs using the various sources and channels available despite the one-dimensional nature of TV. This means that the unique monopoly of the media is now lifted. Everyone who has a smartphone and an internet connection is able to broadcast from anywhere. People no longer feel the need to wait for the bulletin of a cable service or a media organization. Any person who broadcasts or publishes about the event or case they are interested in is now treated in the same way as the journalist or the media of the past. As this monopoly has been destroyed, the structure of schools and education has also changed thoroughly. Today's students are now easily able to reach information that they previously obtained through their teachers at school, using various sources.

Education has always been a field that is contemplated. An interesting study is the utopic monastery Thélème, described by François Rabelais in the 16th century. Rabelais brought a new point of view to the concept of education with this work. In this description, promising men and women living in the monastery who were selected on certain criteria pass through a special education, and can marry, work and visit or leave the monastery as they please.

Enough with the campus and diploma fetish!

In order to compare the old educator and school approach and the new one, I would like to talk about a situation I encountered in high school. When we were coming towards the end of high school education in the late 1980s, not only I, but all my classmates experienced some nervousness about our future and our career plans. Although we received a good high school education, our future was dependent on a three-hour university entrance exam. Istanbul Saint Joseph High School, which I graduated from, was traditionally successful in fields related to positive sciences such as mathematics, physics and chemistry. The aim was to sustain this tradition, but on the other hand, the new world was also starting to present social sciences as an important orientation for a career. Therefore, I and many friends like me were planning to pursue social sciences and have careers in fields such as political science, law, business administration and tourism. However, the school's administration did not agree with us. Instead of the social science classes that we needed for both the exam and general preparation for our careers, they believed all the class should have mathematics, physics and chemistry classes, and they achieved their aim. As a result of their insistence that everyone should graduate from the field of mathematics, our last year in high school turned into a nightmare. If I am not mistaken, in the last year, 42 out of 65 graduates had to take makeup exams in physics, chemistry and mathematics; some did not even succeed in these exams, and we were able to continue university studies at the last moment with the final chance we got. Who knows how many of us experienced dramatic changes in our careers and journeys in life as a result of this imposition, this insistence. I am sure similar impositions have been experienced in other schools and geographies. These obsessions and compulsions of the industrial society are, of course, out of question now in the Information Society.

Schools have been trying experiments for adaptation and usage of new technologies in the current education system since the Information Revolution. Teachers have started to provide the existing content that has been carried into the digital environment for students who use devices such as computers in environments that are known as "smart classrooms". Yet schools and the education system that have on the needs of the industrial society do not seem to have internalized the dynamics of the Digital Revolution as much as new students have. Many large educational institutions think that it is enough to transfer their content into an online environment. However, just as in online marketing, the dynamics of online education are very different from those of traditional methods.

As a clearer example, if you remember the first periods when magazines were transferred to a virtual environment, pages of magazines were placed on the screen as they are in the physical environment, and the sound of turning a page accompanied the motion on the screen. As it was thought at first that magazine covers and the motion of the eyes on the screen overlapped, it was expected while designing websites that the eyes would view the webpage in a Z-shaped pattern just as in the case of a magazine cover. However, as a result of the research conducted by firms such as Tobii who are experts in this field, it was found that this situation was not at all as expected, and the eyes moved over websites in a much more complicated manner.

---

16 Hill, D. (2010). *About face: the secrets of emotionally effective advertising.* London: Kogan Page.

Dan Hill revealed the pattern followed by the eyes while viewing a website in his work entitled *About Face*. With this work, Hill had opened an important door in the field of website design. Likewise the Danish firm Neuroinc also became a pioneer in the effectiveness of websites by carrying out significant scientific studies in this field. Another important firm in this field is the Swedish firm Tobii.[16]

Unfortunately, educators of today who do not have ICTIQ delay the necessary changes related to content by also negatively affecting parents who have been brought up in the old system. However, phenomena such as providing education absolutely within a campus and students attaining master's degrees after graduation, do not go beyond being fetishes within the new educational dynamics of the Information Society. Besides, some lines of work that emerged with the Information Revolution do not even require a university diploma. So far, people have been trained on the basis of the needs of the industrial society, and master's degree programs have been structured on this basis. After a point, employment started to be concerned less with what the person could do, but more with their diploma. Both their school and graduate degree became a label that helped the student find a job after school. However, people who can use information correctly and have ICTIQ and internalized information are more desirable in the Information Society. In this case, the things a person can do in the company they work for with the skills they have undermine their possession of a diploma. The education of people who have been deprived of the skills required by the Information Society and started a job after graduation unfortunately falls into the hands of companies.

The new definition of diploma

If you are using information in the right way in the Information Society, it is possible for you to be successful without having a university diploma. It is enough to look at establishments such as Kickstarter (www.kickstarter.com), where inventors or entrepreneurs present and find funds for projects in various fields from dance to fashion, design to photography, in order to understand where the issue of diploma stands in the Information Society. When you look at the projects on this website, you see that a considerable number of people whose ideas get funded do not have a university diploma. On the other hand, naturally, this is not a healthy indicator. This is because the ratio of people who are successful on such a platform without the necessary education is not high at all. Besides, when education is

---

Neuronsinc; https://www.neuronsinc.com/
Tobii: https://www.tobii.com/

compromised for a project that becomes unsuccessful later, it is more difficult to take care of the negative situation that is caused by the difference created.

Especially in countries such as the USA, we are now witnessing the prevalence of online certificate programs (*self-pickup* certificates) that are designed for lines of work that do not require a university diploma, namely the field of Massive Open Online Courses (MOOC). The American National Education System brought about the obligation to provide thirty percent of all content online for educational institutions in the country. Prominent universities in the United States such as Harvard and MIT are now providing online certificate programs in certain fields for very affordable prices. For example, the free online network of education Coursera (www.coursera.org), which was founded by two academics from Stanford University, is a magnificent platform to reach the best educational content in the world for everyone. On the other hand, although registering for Coursera is easy, being able to follow and complete the courses presented there and utilize the advantages provided on this platform requires good ICTIQ skills.

Today, a university student who wants to be a baker does not necessarily have to get a university diploma. Such a student has the chance to start their business with an online baking certificate that has good content without the need for an academic career. People who are familiar with these programs may access courses by improving their ICTIW skills. However, it is clear that people who are unfamiliar or not able to use the system correctly will be subjected to Digicrimination.

How the content of education evolves

While such important changes are experienced in the world's educational system, it might still not be possible to access similar online programs in some countries, including Turkey. In addition to staying behind in terms of following these developments, we are even failing to make additions onto the current system. As an example, a very important subject like sports communication is still not taught as a separate field in the communications departments of universities. While video games that are accessed via computers or mobile devices have turned into a billion-dollar industry, universities still do not restructure their departments in a way to train programmers and designers who will work in this field. Parents who are uninformed about these new developments and sectors, on the other hand, force their children to receive education in the old system, unknowingly play into the hands of educational institutions that want to preserve the status quo, and jeopardize the future of their children.

Changes in parallel to the Information Revolution are experienced not only in higher education, but also in the content of education that takes place in primary schools, secondary schools and high schools. While the technological capacities of schools and students are being increased, new organizations are simultaneously arranged with consideration of the speed of the virtual world and the concepts of mobility. Countries like Finland, Germany and Japan not only consider this issue to a great extent, but they also make huge investments. For example, students in different age groups in Germany receive part of their education outside the school by visiting certain parts of the city, train stations, parks and museums with their teachers. Just as in Finland, in Japan attention is paid for children to receive education while playing games simultaneously, and this education to be provided without locking children into a classroom or a campus. In Japan, teachers take children to a park and leave them there to play games. The teacher occasionally joins the children and gives a lecture. Children who want to participate listen to the teacher while children who do not continue playing.

Position of the educator against the new student profile

Before looking at what sort of changes are to be made in the school and education system, there is use in knowing about the new generation of students that was trained in the last two decades where the Information Revolution started and gained momentum. We know that this new student profile is in compliance with the speed of the Digital Revolution and able to follow multiple screens and sources of information simultaneously. These students, who naturally have the habit of constantly looking at different channels and following the flow of the digital world, also perceive education differently. Therefore it is important that the contents of classes are structured for students who find it difficult to focus on a subject for a long time. Today, the class duration in many institutions that sustain the classical education system is an undivided forty-five minutes. This duration is actually a length of time that was thought out and determined by the industrial society a long time ago. It is really unreasonable to plan forty-five-minute classes when now scientists are emphasizing that the attention span of the new generation is limited to six or seven minutes.

Even if the duration of classes is shortened, it is a must that the provided content is dynamic. This is because the new generation is now used to following and learning content with visual materials like images and videos, using CBDs and mobile devices. It is highly difficult for dynamic brains to listen to classes that are held with monotonous lectures and learn anything from these classes. Additionally, it is undeniable that we are living in an economic order where not every student has to get a diploma. In such an order, educators should be able to monitor the skills of children of young ages properly, and direct them to the most innovative and practical model of education based on their skills.

> *One of the best examples of this issue may be followed in the TED Talk by British academic Ken Robinson.*
> *(https://www.ted.com/talks/ken_robinson_says_schools_kill_creativity)*

On the other hand, with the globalization brought about by the Information Revolution, global values are continuing to integrate with local values. It is now inevitable to provide global cultures alongside local values in the education system of a country. Whether it is economically developed or not, every young person in a country with internet access knows what Masala or Sushi is. The game Angry Birds is known in all corners of the world. While people are talking about the world today as a global village, we are able to see that the situation will go even further than this culture. Therefore, we may comfortably say that the demands on the content of education will change in parallel to this in the near future. In the following years, with the popularized usage of Virtual Reality technologies in education, there will be no use for cadavers in medical training, for instance. Chemical experiments will be presented to students in an interesting way in 3D. The question that arises here is this: are educators able to train teachers who will be able to provide this and contribute to students in the new educational ecosystem? Unfortunately, if we answer this question based on the current state of affairs, it is no.

Many educators who are used to the old order including the classical education system and schools are choosing the easy way and resisting the creation of new content and development of a different language of communication to interact with their students. While the things said by the teacher were completely accepted as the truth in the past, with the internet, students started to question what they were told and access whatever they need immediately. This situation tarnished the authority of the current model of educator in the classroom to a great extent. The student has found the opportunity to watch the application of the subject taught in a chemistry class immediately by looking at YouTube. In summary, while the school is no longer the one indisputable factor for education alongside the media, the old model of educators is now becoming history. That is, importance is now being paid to the educator transmitting knowledge in the classroom by following the developments in the Information Society. Additionally, educators now have to leave the didactic "I know all" attitude aside and adopt the model of a teacher who guides students and directs them on the basis of their skills.

In a project that I participated in some time ago as a consultant, we asked the teachers of a prestigious high school to provide opinions without any limitations to design the education of the future. What we observed in the presentations made by the teachers was that they presented recommendations that did not go beyond the current order in order to not lose their current statuses and values. I think this micro-example has a counterpart on a macroscale.

Of course, the chance to immediately access the subjects that are taught in the class on the internet led to a misconception among some students as "I do not need school. I can learn about everything via the internet." Although today's students are able to access any subject they want in an instant, they are having difficulty with in-depth learning, comprehension and interpretation of that subject in case they are not able to internalize the information they have received. One of the greatest problems that educators experience is getting through to this group of students that I have frequently observed in my academic experiences and call Dignorant (Digital Ignorant). An educator, in addition to having in-depth knowledge of the subject they are teaching, should also be alert to this misconception that students may fall into. They should communicate with the students in the same language, and produce new methods for them to do research and acquire in-depth learning. Utilizing new technologies for the new generation of students to listen to and learn in classes with pleasure makes the job of educators easier. Unfortunately, Dignorant students who think they learn everything via the internet keep away from new education models such as online certificate programs, and they do not even know what kind of an opportunity they are missing. Providing information in this matter is, once again, the job of educators.

I think the case of seeing ignorance as acceptable has now become usual. The American writer and biochemist Isaac Asimov summarized this so well: "The impact of anti-intellectualism on our political and cultural life is rooted in the misconception that says, 'my ignorance is as good as your knowledge'." The belief that ignorance is an acceptable or cool characteristic once again confronts humanity with the Information Revolution, but now is much stronger. [17]

---

17 Isaac Asimov, (21 January 1980) "A Cult of Ignorance", Newsweek, January 1980, p. 19.

The issue of missing life while going to school

There is a considerable proportion of students in today's education system who think going to school is not good for anything. The difference between fast-flowing social media or the virtual world and the education system in real life leads students to experience the Digital Schizophrenia that I frequently mentioned here. In this case, the main problem experienced by the school and the educator is the mindset of the student who has been exposed to the phenomenon of Digital Schizophrenia. If we compare the situation with the past, the school used to be a center of attraction regardless of the level. While students had been saying "I miss a lot when I don't go to school" till twenty years ago, they have now come to say "I miss a lot when I go to school". Going to school and receiving an education is completely meaningless for this group of students. Young people who think there is something completely different happening in the world while they are taught in the classroom and they miss life while at school lose their motivation without being informed about the danger they will face while building their future.

Screen Addiction affects learning modality

If the content provided for children by the teacher or their parents and the way of providing this content are not more interesting than what the student finds on the screen, it becomes almost impossible to communicate with the student. Screen Addiction prevents students from establishing a relationship with people around them. The sad part of the issue is that this problem usually remains unnoticed as the teachers or parents themselves are also screen-addicted. This situation is a serious problem that must be overcome both in daily life and in the education system. The student whose direct communication with people diminishes due to Screen Addiction in addition to constantly accessing visual materials in the virtual world has started to speak with fewer words. Young people who have got used to communication with emojis or symbols are losing their vocabulary and some concepts. For example, instead of saying "anthracite color", they are saying "this color" and losing their skills of description.

If the student only has a textbook to study from, it becomes harder to understand the subject that is taught. Young people who read their magazines and books digitally, like the subject with one click when needed and share or remove things on demand, confuse the conditions of physical books and the screen, and lag behind. As they access several pieces of information from unknown sources on the internet, they are having difficulty in reaching the right source and providing citations. As they are able to reach everything in the digital environment, they do not make an effort to keep anything in their minds, and therefore they cannot take part in a debate in the classroom or produce arguments.

I am a person who thinks we need to use time effectively. I can say, based on my observations, that there is an old habit in the academic world that needs to be changed. As every word of academics is listened to with great care when they deliver lectures traditionally or talk about their subject of expertise for any reason, their belief in the importance of a need for acceptance of what they say is very high. Maybe academics in the period up to the 1990s were on such a level that, when they talked about their area of expertise, they were able to attract interest in the audience they addressed and contribute to them with something new. They were able to provide the audience with information, experiences and analyses that they had never heard of. This made what academics said more interesting. Thus they had content for hours of speech and audiences that would listen to them for hours. After the Information Revolution and content accessed through the internet based on this, the audiences of these academics, including students, were faced with various new contents in the same subject. In a way, the monopoly of academics on information and analysis was broken, or even destroyed. Academics witnessed a new case that they had to compete with, and they were caught off guard. Unfortunately, most of them continued to think that what they said was very important, instead of changing their habits and making what they said interesting to sui an environment of competition, refreshing themselves or improving their qualifications. Their impunity went on through panels that were known to be boring, unchanged content and hours of meetings that resulted in nothing. Moreover, for one reason or another, academic institutions also continued to revere the academics who were evaluated by the old criteria of measurement. The new generation which was stuck in this situation, bored by an education that had now become bland, and not able to concentrate, started to receive information from the digital world. Even worse, they started to think that they learned this information. Naturally, their qualifications stayed insufficient due to incomplete information. Academics, on the other hand, indicated the learning modality of the new generation as the reason for this issue.

In one of the institutions I worked at, a panel discussion was organized at 7:00 pm on a Saturday without any attraction factor in terms of both the content and the speakers. To make attendance at the panel obligatory, low doses of professional mobbing were imposed on the educators for a week. Based on the information I received after the panel, attendance at the panel was low, and each of the speakers who were initially given twenty minutes of time spoke for about ninety minutes. I am sure these speakers were thinking that what they were saying was very interesting. Some students attended to gain approval, some academics attended to gain the approval of the administration, and some attended because they had nothing better to do. What was the result? Who cares! Everyone had their ego satisfied.

We see that the view of the business world or namely the practical world on the academic world has overwhelmingly become negative in the last twenty years because of academics who cannot renew themselves and are practically living on another planet. In this case, what is said by prominent academics, their analyses that should be considered with care, comments and warnings, have turned out to be for nothing.

In summary, in the Information Society we are living in, this education model that is left over from the industrial society certainly does not achieve sustainability, but is almost being destroyed. It is doomed to be destroyed anyway. Transitivity is increasing among disciplines that have up to now been far from each other with the new business models that have emerged. In addition to this, technology is increasingly bringing social sciences and positive sciences together. For example, new profiles such as industrial engineers who know psychology become needed. While educators who do not have ICTIQ are becoming outdated on one hand, education content needs to be renewed based on students who can multitask on the other hand. Based on all these, while the fetish of diploma and campus is ending, online education programs are gaining momentum. It would be wrong to say that no difficulties arise despite these positive trends. While Digital Schizophrenia and Screen Addiction make skills of learning and analysis stiffer, the prevalence of CBD and mobile application usage in education and the issue of unfair distribution not only create inequality, but also foster Digicrimination.

Recommendations for a new education model: Everything must change from scratch!

The walls of the education building constructed based on the needs of the industrial society are starting to come down; the building is now being shaken to its foundations. It worries me as an academic to see that, despite this situation, educators or parents are still not searching for ways of not leaving the new generation in the ruins. With the effects of the Information Revolution, the generation gap between today's children and young people and our generation is wider than a gap of one generation. However, whatever happens, we must accept that we need to experience a revolutionary transformation, and start reconstruction right away. Nowadays, there is an approach in the education system of various countries including Turkey that mainly changes some topics of the curriculum and says, "let this course stay and that one go." Debates like which of the mathematics and philosophy courses are more important are now both outdated and unnecessary. The educational content of the period we are living in goes far beyond these superficial debates. It is now a necessity to create educational content defined with the technology of today that is designed not only for life, but also for training students who will easily adapt to a life that will change again in the near future and use the education they receive effectively. Hence, everything in the current education system as we know it should change.

However strongly educators and parents may resist to sustain the old order, change is inevitable. Students in the new generation are already in this change and they are growing up internalizing all kinds of developments. However, restructuring of the system is only in the hands of institutions and parents, that is, decision-makers. Thus, legislators and decision-makers in particular should pay attention to recommendations regarding education. It would be unjust and pure imagination to expect that educational institutes and educators will act to improve themselves before such people take determined steps towards change.

Not fun education, but education suitable for the new learning method

Whenever issues such as developing content suitable for the Age of Information and renewing the education system are opened up to debate in the field of education, we are frequently seeing recommendations towards making content more fun. Such a recommendation is based on the prevalence of mobility, and access to information on the digital environment by the new generation mostly through videos, visual materials or social media. However, when education is considered, it is not always possible to provide the content in a fun way. In this case, it is important to prepare the content and the education system in consideration of the habits and learning methods of the new generation.

We know that students today prefer new devices such as digital books instead of traditional books. Therefore, while developing a new education system, it is critically important to use CBDs effectively and appropriately in the field of education. On the other hand, the main problem here is the mindset that sees the intersection of the digital world and education as merely limited to use of tablets or computers in classrooms.

When we look at the technologies developed for the field of education, we see that learning methods from before the Information Revolution were taken as a basis at first. For example, while developing software for Kindle, inspiration was taken from physical books, and features that belong to traditional reading habits such as the sound of turning pages were added to the application. This was actually an effort to sustain the old order. However, with the development of mobile technologies followed by the emergence of applications for learning, we are now at a new stage in this issue. Mobile applications have made book-reading and information -gathering methods different. For example, if we consider applications for learning a foreign language such as Rosetta Stone, Duolingo or FluentU, we see educational tools that pay attention to new visual-based learning methods and cognitive modalities where content may be used more effectively. The most important characteristics of such applications are their infrastructures which use multimedia very well.

We started to use our visual and auditory memories more intensely with the entry of mobile technology into our lives. We are having difficulty registering topics that we do not hear or see. This is even more difficult for the new generation born into the Information Revolution and used to accessing content this way. Therefore it is not fair to expect that students will learn anything by reading only, even in a technological environment. This development brought some learning methods that were previously not appreciated much back into attention, like the Michael Thomas method that proposes learning a language by memorizing sentences instead of focusing on grammar... Educational systems such as the techniques of keeping information in the mind and improving memory proposed by Paul Noble started to be reintegrated into education.

I learned French, English and Spanish in secondary school, high school and university. It is naturally easier to learn a language at an early age rather than a later age. I experienced many problems when I started learning German in my mid-forties. However, in this case, I could access dozens of different opportunities developed fir individuals with different profiles. Additionally, there are applications such as Tandem where everyone is an amateur teacher in the language they speak and a student in the language they are trying to learn, people meet on the internet, gather at a suitable time and reinforce their practical knowledge. Websites which provide language teaching for people located in different places through applications such as Skype are also very popular. Of course, just as in all other fields of Digicrimination, there arises a difference between those who can use this and those who cannot.

It has already become old-fashioned to make presentations in classrooms with PowerPoint, which was the "latest technology" of the past. Instead, students are more interested in making their presentations with interactive applications such as Video Scribe. That is, of course, if the educator has an awareness about presenting the topics they are teaching in this way, and has reached sufficiency in ICTIQ... Likewise, if an academic teaching in the field of architecture has never used devices like Doodle that create three-dimensional drawings, they will not think of having their students use them. On the contrary, it is not in their interests to dive into uncharted waters. Unfortunately, educators prefer blaming other stakeholders in education instead of improving themselves.

Nowadays, with the addition of new CBDs on tools used in classrooms such as tablets, computers and smartboards, it has become possible to access a very diverse set of applications. Via a CBD, you can turn a normal computer screen that you use in the classroom into a touch screen in an instant. Moreover, CBDs are doors to the world of widely varying applications. For example, regardless of location in the world, an engineering student is able to reach a mathematics application, and an architecture student is able to reach applications that make three-dimensional drawing easier. This makes such students different. The Digicrimination I mentioned is exactly like this. As applications like Periscope are now able to provide live broadcasts with dynamic flows using such applications, any student can broadcast the class live for a friend who was not able to attend that day.

Digital books have now turned into technologies called Augmented Books where images or experiments on the page can be followed in three dimensions and with auditory support. In addition to being highly useful in a pedagogic sense, this technology also leads students to learn by having fun. For example, a tree on a coloring-book page becomes three-dimensional with the help of a video that was previously uploaded; the carousel in another page becomes live and starts rotation as soon as the child completes the coloring process. With *augmented* books, a student who wants to learn about the ideas of famous Communication Academic Marshall McLuhan in the class they are taking will not only listen to a lecture by McLuhan himself, but also will get the chance to view lecture notes holographically. In addition to educational institutes, *augmented* books have now started to be used by large firms too. For example, an automobile firm or a chain of supermarkets prefers to use this technology in their catalogues.

As a social sciences person, when I saw smartphone applications such as PhotoMath and Mathway for the first time I could not believe my eyes. Then, of course, I could not help but think how having such an opportunity in my days as a student could change my life.

Recommendations for restructuring in education

After all this problem assessment, I think it would be right to present a few recommendations for education to be restructured in a way that suits the necessities of the Age of Information. First of all, in order to change an education system that was designed for the needs of the industrial society as soon as possible, political decision-makers, educators, educational institutions and especially parents should start acting together. In this context, it is now inevitable that the old education system will be changed from top to bottom and Digital Revolution and mobility-compliant education methods will be established. The important thing here is the formation of a long-term plan that will keep up with the speed of the new era, adapt itself to situations fast, and ensure that the system will be dynamically restructured in a few years. A new education system may be formed based on this plan. This new system should be designed not on the basis of campuses or in-class activities as in the past, but with the aim of making presentation possible in different digital environments including mobile ones. Accordingly, the obses-sion with diplomas, master's degrees and campuses should be left behind. The environment where education will be provided should be transformed to become a suitable place for the era. Without repeating the mistakes of today's system, a search should start for the ways to stay up to date for technologies that are used for education today and those that may be used in the future. To achieve this, close contact should be established with technology firms, programmers and various education experts. On the other hand, new business models that are developing should be followed and parents and students should be informed about these areas. In this way, it will be ensured that the student will be successful not only in education but also in professional life, and advance in professions that are compli-ant with personal characteristics. This is because it is possible that students and parents who are uninformed about new business fields will make big mistakes. Of course, in order to achieve such an ideal situation, ICTIQ skills for educators and academics should be improved and educators should be supported with the right methods. While doing this, it would be a great approach to consider the feedback of students on the content and way of presentation of classes. Addition-ally, in order for them to improve the skills of analysis and information filtering which are highly important in the Information Society, it is essential to improve the skills of students, which will lead them to acquire in-depth learning about information that they reach easily. Transferring some part of educational content into an online environment and development of new certificate programs are now also a necessity regardless of the field of education.

The first step for all these may be to give up imposing clichéd ways of education. Regarding the field in which they have been providing education from pre-school to university levels, educators should not only have intellectual knowledge, but they should also follow learning methods and technologies that will help them provide this information. While doing this, it is a necessity to give up being the person who just provides information and teaches it, and evolve into a role that directs students. As I have mentioned again and again, content is important in education. So is the readiness of the educator for the competitive environment... Therefore, while presenting the content to be taught, an educator should utilize memory improvement techniques and visual/auditory learning methods.

While books with Augmented Reality properties, dynamic multimedia presentation tools like VideoScribe and Prezi, CBDs that improve current technologies used in the classroom and specific applications designed for engineering, architecture and even medicine exist and are already being used, it is not just a necessity but an obligation to have students use these effectively. The focus of students' attention can only be kept in the classroom environment with these dynamic and interesting pieces of content.

There is a need to emphasize a point beyond all these predictions and recommendations about education. There is a dominant view that online education will not satisfy the need for trained labor in areas that are very specific and require more technical details and a wider knowledge base, especially such as engineering. As I am not even close to these fields, I cannot share a comment. People who are working in these fields will provide better answers to the questions about what the qualities are that people who are trained in these fields that require long years of heavy education should have, and how these qualities may be obtained. However, if not in the current situation, I would speculate that all fields will face an online education revolution in the long run with changing and developing online education technologies.

End of the reluctant seller and new entrepreneurship

We mentioned that humankind has designed a new education system that is suitable for the conditions of the age it has lived in since the day it started developing. However, the history of entrepreneurship does not go as far back as education. Whenever the concepts of commerce and shopping entered our daily lives, we then started to talk about "entrepreneurs". Today's entrepreneurship is rooted in the transition to the industrial society. While we were living in the agricultural society before, our priority was survival. It was sufficient for us to satisfy our basic needs such as shelter and eating/drinking. The phenomena of obtaining a raw material and processing it, acquiring a product and delivering the product to people in exchange for a price arose as values that belonged to the industrial society. Following this process, we encountered new concepts such as marketing. Various marketing methods were developed for selling a product to wider consumer bases. For example, Coca Cola, which was being sold as a painkiller for headaches, started to be sold as a beverage in time by following the attention paid by the consumers, and reached our time in this way. Coca Cola, which attracted attention as a beverage, gained such huge marketing and advertising power that even Santa Claus, who originally wore green, is still associated with the color red as he was depicted wearing this color in Coca Cola advertisements.

The industrial society, as opposed to the type of production in the agricultural society, established a completely product-oriented structure. Workers who were walking around in the factory during production in early times started to work at the end of the conveyor-belt after the automotive giant Ford initiated this model for the first time. Each worker had a certain job; sometimes one worker was responsible for tightening the same screw all day. With these implementations, we witnessed the emergence of concepts such as alienation of the workers from the products they produce. We occasionally see TV footages of workers where they sort out the products on a moving belt, choose and pack them up, and are able to do this at top speed with their advanced manual skills. Whenever I see these footages, I imagine myself in front of that belt, and think I would not be able to sustain the concentration shown by the workers for a long time. My respect for those workers increases even further when I think that they are doing this for hours, days and even weeks.

In those periods, it was very hard to obtain raw materials due to limited transportation opportunities and the limited number of highways. While it corresponds to the last phases of the industrial society, even the establishment of the European Union (EU) was based on overcoming these harsh conditions. With the EU (European Economic Community, to use its first name) that was designed as a platform for economic collaboration, it was actually planned to establish easy movement of the raw material steel, which was very hard to achieve at the time. As the Russian and Eastern European markets were closed to commerce due to the political conditions of the time, it became a necessity to form a collaboration platform to obtain raw materials and present the products on the market. In short, raw materials and products were the top priorities of economies till the end of the 20th century.

I do not know if you would also remember those days, but it was a big deal to obtain a certain product in the Turkey of my childhood due to limited production and weak economic infrastructure. In 1970s, in order to obtain a high-quality product, say a pair of jeans, people would visit the American Market in Karaköy, Istanbul. Of course, if they had the purchasing power to buy that product... I never forget this: when we bought a Wrangler brand pair of blue jeans with a high price tag from the American Market for my older brother in those years, our cousins, friends and many others visited our home to see those jeans. While this story looks funny today, it is actually understandable when one considers the difficulty of obtaining products and insufficient purchasing power at that time. All commercial relationships and entrepreneurship dynamics were structured on the basis of those conditions. As the product was of the greatest value, sellers would assign whatever price they wanted for it. Additionally, many products could only be bought in certain stores because of the state monopoly and regulations.

I remember that in the 1970s, as a family, we would frequently visit the stores of Sümerbank, which used to possess a monopoly in fabric and textile products. Sümerbank, which was a state establishment, was selling domestic and high-quality products for affordable prices. Anyway, store employees working there would completely reflect the market conditions of the period. I remember that, once, when my mother wanted to look at a fabric on the shelf closely, the salesperson told her "I'll take it down if you're going to buy it, or else don't make me tired." Similar experiences introduced the concept of the "reluctant seller" into our daily language at the time.

> Car sellers and real estate agents in Germany in 2016 are all in this category. The salesperson whom I told that I would like to buy a car not caring about my appointment, and the response I received in an empty dealership: "we are busy today, go to another dealership", are all results of this outdated approach.

When the share of the product in total value decreases

While this order was ongoing in the market, we experienced the intersection of three significant developments that I mentioned in previous sections in the 1990s: strengthening of communication by the development in international relations, commerce made easier, and the internet starting to be used. With the Information Revolution, it became easier for products and services to spread. With increased movement, there came an abundance of products in the market, and it also became possible to market products and services by reaching the furthest corners of the world via the internet. Commerce, economic relationships, investment and financing activities, money markets, entrepreneurship and all connected factors experienced this change.

For example, the price of red marble, which used to be a very rare and expensive product in the past, started to decline after Italian designers started to reach producers all around the world. Wrangler jeans, which people made home visits to observe in the past, can now be found everywhere. While the value of commercial products which became accessible with the Digital Revolution in the economy decreased, various services have become alternatives to products. In shorter terms, dominance of the product in the total added value ended, together with the reluctant seller.

At this point, everyone from banks and similar large establishments to the smallest retailer or producer had to adapt to the new environment. While websites acted as store windows where companies shared information and showcased their products in the first years of internet usage in commerce, the products and services provided lost their attractiveness in time.

What makes what you are selling unique?

When product abundance and decreases in the old values of products were experienced with the Information Revolution, as consumers we all started to ask the sellers the following question: "What makes your product or service different, unique?" In an instant, the reluctant seller changed his attitude, and started to say "the customer is always right." The customer utilized this opportunity well and started to use the power of platforms on digital platforms for sharing criticisms, experiences and other details about the firms.

The milestone for the effectiveness of customer complaints was the musician Dave Carroll's video titled *United broke my guitar* against United Airlines in US. The video was watched on Youtube by millions and had a big impact. This sharing broke new ground in carrying customer complaints into the online environment.

Pandora's Box was opened at once, and the question that no one wanted to hear reached all ears. It became important that there was a feature of a product or service that madeit different from others and provides competitive advantage, a Unique Selling Proposition provided by the seller to the customer. The entrepreneur profiles that we knew so far changed forever in this way.

What is waiting for the traditional seller?

In the beginning of the Information Revolution, companies and entrepreneurs tried to continue the traditional way of doing business by putting their business online. However, in a short time, the virtual world started to impose its own dynamics and ways of doing business. It became important to have ICTIQ skills. For today's entrepreneurs, having ICTIQ is not just a necessity, but an obligation. If the entrepreneur does not have a unique product or service, they need to know how to differentiate their product, and use social media and mobile applications effectively.

If the entrepreneur is not a producer but, for example, just a shopkeeper selling glasses, it is important for them to achieve success without following the trends in the digital world. Glasses with wooden frames may be popular today and this trend my affect sales positively for some time. However, if the glasses seller falls behind in following the trends in the digital world, prices and new models, their profitability will diminish in a short time.

Since the earliest period of the Information Revolution, the digital world has been continuing to impose its own dynamics and evolve. When entrepreneurs and people who are involved in economic activity started production and transferring their goods via the internet fast, some people started to have difficulties between the speed of activity in the real world and the speed brought about by the virtual world. Failure of official regulations to keep up with the speed of the virtual world, bureaucratic processes that required printed documents, failure to establish a legal basis for transactions that take place in the virtual environment and ongoing offline habits led to congestions and issues in operations. This way, entrepreneurs were also introduced to Digital Schizophrenia. Additionally, we witnessed how many entrepreneurs tried to transfer the traditional business model exactly as it was onto the web, use advertisements that were designed for print media and TV dynamics on the internet, or, in other words, try to integrate apples and oranges. However, the genuine structure of the digital world showed us that this effort is futile in many cases. Think about the disproportionate number of digital advertising agencies that emerged with the prevalence of websites. There were many organizations that wanted to post advertisements on the internet via advertising firms that are actually used to produce advertisements for traditional media but call themselves digital agencies just for the sake of complying with the trend. All these trials resulted in failure. In particular sellers who did not have a valuable product had even more difficulties with the new developments. It seems that these difficulties will continue in the following periods.

Opening a store, not a website for prestige

As already mentioned, one of the important books by Malcolm Gladwell, *David and Goliath*, talked about how the fighting powers of small-scale firms that are trying to survive by considering the dynamics of the industrial society in the crushing conditions of capitalism changed in comparison with larger structures. While this book was written recently, what would its title be if it were written a few years later, in today's conditions? "Heroic company against the virtual platform," maybe? All joking aside, transferring the business world into the virtual environment actually provided important advantages for the heroic shopkeeper of the past-if, of course, this shopkeeper was following the dynamics of the Digital Revolution and reforming the business on this basis.

Today, almost all companies are paying attention to their presence on the internet, and not acting without organizing a website or a mobile site. Many new companies operate on the internet only, with the advantages provided by this. The kiosk that brought food to our homes by taking orders over the phone is being replaced by *yemeksepeti.com*. We may say that significant awareness of this matter is now in place in the business world. This is really great news. However, this has become such an obsession for some that some companies have almost fetishized the appearance of their website and the technology they use. These firms are so much involved in the details of their websites or mobile applications that they may forget to focus on the priorities required by their businesses. If we leave this negative habit aside, we may see the direction in which the business world is heading, the actual picture. Today's entrepreneurs consider the costs of operating a business in a physical environment and turn all possible operations digital. With the continuation of this trend, the "heroic shopkeeper" will take on another task in the next few years. Companies operating in the physical environment used to set up a website just for prestige. Websites were used as store windows to showcase the products and services of the company. However, the situation has now been reversed; stores in the physical environment are taking up the task of creating prestige for companies. Apple stores are a great example of this. Soon not only technology firms like Apple but other companies that sell completely different products will also follow the same path.

The website *yemeksepeti.com*, which valued development from the first day of its establishment, provided food--ordering services, gathered restaurants, kiosks and similar firms together, and became successful with a fine filtering method and user-friendly interface, was sold to a firm named Delivery Hero in 2015 for $589 million. For a firm that is involved in industrial production to be sold at this price, how much success should it achieve, and what should its turnover and size be?[18]

---

18 Delivery Hero Buys Middle East Web Food Service for $589 Million. (2015, May 05). Retrieved October 27, 2017, from https://www.bloomberg.com/news/articles/2015-05-05/delivery-hero-buys-middle-east-web-food-service-for-589-million

The best thing that can be done by the traditional seller or entrepreneur would be to cooperate with consultants with ICTIQ who will draw a road map, help determine the right target audience, and reach this audience.

Changing economic ecosystem and neuromarketing

On the other hand, changes in the world's economic ecosystem directed entrepreneurs to find and implement new sales and marketing methods. At this point, neuroscience became one of the fields that came to the help of entrepreneurs. This field of science, which is focused on discovering the human mind, is acting towards developing marketing techniques that are suitable for our perceptions by creating a map of our mental behaviors. Neuromarketing, which developed with the support of this field, helps companies monitor how consumers decide while making purchases in a scientific way and develop marketing strategies about this.

In my opinion, neuromarketing is the biggest evidence that the discrimination created by the digital age is not only on a personal but also on an institutional level. The difference between the firms that have this opportunity and are able to use it and those who do not is so large that it would not be wrong to define this situation as discrimination.

In 2002, scientists named Daniel Kahneman and Amos Tversky conducted a study which revealed that people do not make rational decisions while shopping, and, on the contrary, they make decisions based on a set of prejudices and subconscious shortcuts. After this research received the Nobel Prize in Economics in the same year, the idea of behavioral economics started to gain attention throughout the entire world. This paved the way for similar studies.

As neuroscience advanced, naturally, neuromarketing also became a field that advanced in the light of this. Undeniably, neuroscience assumed a pioneering role in both the scientific world and the corporate world as a way of discovering the human mind.

Books such as *Buyology, Brandsense*, written by the marketing management expert Martin Lindstrom, had a big influence on the changing experience in the fields of communication and marketing in the last decade[19]. In his book *Buyology*, Lindstrom showed that most shopping is done on the basis of influence of emotions rather than needs. Dan Hill developed technology that makes it possible to do market research with a face recognition system. With the scoring method

---

19 Lindström, M. (2010). *Buy•ology: truth and lies about why we buy*. New York: Broadway Books. Lindström, M. (2010). *Brand sense: build powerful brands through touch, taste, smell, sight and sound*. London: Kogan Page.

he developed, he managed to turn face recognition into a functioning market research method.

Another name among the experts who made a significant mark in this field is one of the world's prominent communication and advertising consultants, Clotaire Rapaille. With his work titled *The Culture Code,* Rapaille investigated how people's personalities differ. *The Culture Code* shows ways to find answers to questions such as "what do people buy while shopping?' and even "how one can determine with whom people fall in love?". In this book, Rapaille states that these answers are hidden in culture codes.

Another scientist who investigates the effects of logic and emotions in decision-making mechanisms is Antonio Damasio. Neurologist Dr. Damasio, who starts with experiences from patients with brain damage, explained how damage to emotions and feelings disrupted the functioning of the mind and social behaviors. His work named *Descartes' Error,* which changed the perception of the relationship between the body and the mind in a revolutionary way, has become an inspiration for psychologists who developed the concept of emotional intelligence.[20]

Thus, the entrepreneurs of the Age of Information found new marketing techniques, sales methods and technologies that would provide them with advantages in the market.

One of the hardest-hitting questions of marketing is: "from where and with which techniques do we know what the consumer thinks and how they make decisions?". Today, with the help of neuroscience, this question has answers that have never been clearer. While we are in the stage of decision-making, the neurons in our brain start to work and produce electricity. Because of this, our body needs more blood and our metabolism experiences a change. Neuromarketing is now able to detect this change in the metabolism with the data provided by neuroscience. We can see which parts of our brain work and become activated. As certain parts of the brain have the same functions, for example, we already know which part will be activated while listening to music. This way, the tendencies of the consumer can be monitored by using measurement technologies such as FMRI (Functional Magnetic Resonance Imaging), EEG (Electroencephalography), FC.

Companies have already started to design their platforms in the virtual environment based on the data obtained as a result of such studies. Designs that are known as eye tracking which make tracking of the eyes easier, words and expressions used in texts to attract the consumer, avoidance of using numbers, correct

---

20 Damasio, A. R. (2000). *Descartes error: emotion, reason, and the human brain.* New York: Quill.

and appropriate usage of colors and similar techniques are the gifts of neuro-marketing to us. Apparently, similar studies will continue to provide significant competitive advantages for today's entrepreneurs.

So is there not a difference between those who have this brand-new digital opportunity and use it, and those who do not?

In 2010, I was at a Neuromarketing firm named in Minnesota which is one of the best-known neuromarketing firms not only in the USA but also the world. My aim was to bring the methods of the firms back to Europe and Turkey. While I was being shown sample studies in this context, one of the projects caught my attention. An NBA team was interested in a player, but they asked the firm for the player's "Emotional Profile" before transferring him. Sensory Logic produced the "Emotional Profile" of the player by face reading and sent it to the team. On the basis of the profile revealed, this player did not have the qualities that the team desired. Thus the NBA team decided not to transfer the player. It is a case that is worth a "wow!" I think there is no need for me to say that this method is now being used for candidates who attend job interviews.

Following digital clues

With the Information Revolution, we have started to encounter brand-new business models that we could not even imagine in the period of industrial economy. It took us a very short time to know and internalize social media platforms such as Facebook and Twitter, smartphones or mobile applications that were developed under the lead-ership of Apple, and technologies such as virtual reality. The way these technologies were created aside, some of us are still having difficulty with how these businesses that are not based on tangible products make money. In the approaching new period, we will witness the rapid prevalence of virtual reality, three-dimensional printers and such products. It will be even more difficult to comprehend these concepts.

Yet these new business models continue to appeal to the appetites of many entrepreneurs. When a computer engineer friend of mine with whom I recently had a conversation stated that he was having difficulty in finding programmers to employ, I was very surprised at first. In fact, my friend was talking about the demand for the job, not the deficiency of human resources. I smiled when I heard: "the new generation now wants to develop their own Facebook or game applica-tion and immediately become rich. This is why they do not prefer to work even for prestigious software firms like ours." Maybe it is not possible for everyone to create an ecosystem like Facebook, but I am sure that many entrepreneurs who follow digital clues with today's technology and their ICTIQ skills may very well create new and effective businesses.

What CBDs offer for entrepreneurs

In addition to the internet and social media, usage of CBDs also started to provide brand new opportunities for entrepreneurs. Offline devices that utilize SIM cards or wireless connections such as POS machines, measurement devices, architecture/drawing/engineering devices, screens that show our number in banks, screens in cars, navigation devices, loyalty cards that work on RF and many others... None of these devices is conventionally related to the machine we call a computer. Use of these chip- based devices that were designed to make our life and the service we receive easier in various places from parking lots to shopping malls has led to the accumulation of a significant amount of valuable information called big data in the virtual world. These data provide us with important clues about the habits of consumers. It would not be unreasonable to claim that the entrepreneurs who filter these data correctly, turn them into meaningful data by analysis and package them will shine in the near future. Besides, there is no need to be a software engineer. When they include implementations such as neuromarketing, entrepreneurs who use big data well may create applications that exactly address a consumer need that is very simple but not yet known. They only need to have the necessary informatics infrastructure while organizing their business.

Global warming and environment-friendly technologies

Our world is facing the threat of global warming due to various factors such as brutal consumption of natural resources for years by the industrial economy, the population explosion, and increases in aerial transportation methods. However, the Information Revolution allows us to create a system where we would be able to protect the natural ecosystem by contributing to the development of environment-friendly technologies and energy systems. (You will read about the development of nature-friendly technologies and environmentally responsible energy systems in the following sections that discuss the energy sector.) New developments in this field also present new investment and working fields for entrepreneurs.

Cases and recommendations for entrepreneurs

When access to the products put onto markets around the world became easier with the Information Revolution due to changing commercial conditions, transportation opportunities, internet stores and similar factors, the share of the product in the total economic value decreased. Therefore competition escalated in terms of the product, and naturally, factors such as customer satisfaction, brand value and quality gained more weight in the total economic value. In this case, the "reluctant seller" who previously did not have to make an effort to sell the product had to change. Some made investments in employees and services to adapt to the situation and change. Some are still insisting on staying stuck with their old habits. My personal view is that this obsession cannot continue much longer and all reluctant sellers will surrender in the end.

In addition to this, in the new business environment of the Information Society, while the business models that may be defined as traditional were carried over to the web, the entrepreneur encountered the concept of Digital Schizophrenia and understood that the virtual world had a completely different dynamic. Additionally, awareness was reached about the importance of emphasizing the unique characteristics of a product that makes it different from others, in addition to the importance of having a product. This is because the question asked by the consumer is now very simple: "why should I buy your product?" Besides, contrary to what is usually thought and assumed, price is still very important at the stage of decision-making for many products, but it is not at the top. The consumer is now in search of other things besides the price.

As the relationship with the consumer became increasingly sophisticated, studies conducted with old methods naturally had to be replaced by new ones. By utilizing not only technology but also scientific fields such as neuroscience, new sales and marketing strategies like neuromarketing were developed. When it was demonstrated that people mostly decide with their subconscious, techniques relevant to their subconscious became popular. Brand-new business models that could not even be imagined in the industrial society and its established economic ecosystem have emerged.

Well, what is the direction of affairs?

First of all, it should be noted that the indecision experienced especially by retailers regarding moving from a physical environment to the virtual world has now ended. It is now impossible to survive for firms that have no websites, or those who cannot properly establish relationships over their existing websites. All physical operations are being moved to the virtual environment step by step due to dynamics such as speed and costs. The importance of presence in the digital environment has been understood not only by retail firms but also most companies regardless of their sector, but this time a "website fetish" started. Websites have become the reference and marketing environments of agencies and firms that provide web design services. An approach developed towards imposing their own material and approaches instead of having the user understand the website easily and be able to use and utilize it. Dozens of flashy, visually crowded, complicated but dysfunctional websites, of course, could not achieve the expected effect. The period of "accepting the mediocre and not asking for extra work" that was based on an unwritten agreement between agencies and relevant departments of firms is now over. The days of agencies that modify only the colors and content of the same website design and try to market it to more than a few firms in a day are also over. Firms have now become familiar with the subject to an extent to be able to demand alternative designs and website infrastructures that are simple but effective and will transmit their message to the end user most effectively. This will make the jobs of agencies and designers who are used to ready-made projects more difficult. They now have to satisfy the demands that they have previously blocked by indicating technical limitations as the reason and also achieve customer satisfaction like everybody else.

With implementations such as web-sites, e-mail and similar applications, it has now become an obligation to have ICTIQ and follow developments in the digital world for firms that have to communicate with their audience, and even small-time business people who have shops.

Here, as I mentioned earlier, while digital stores and websites have started to be widely accepted and used, companies that set up a website for prestige in the past now have to redesign the points where consumers will contact them to support their virtual trade while carrying out their business in the virtual environment, open physical stores for prestige, or make their physical spaces consistent with and similar to their activities in the virtual world.

Opportunities for entrepreneurship

There is always an opportunity for a successful business model on the internet. On the other hand, entrepreneurs have to follow the now rapidly changing and transforming trends and find a good model. My personal view is that, in the near future, people will be able to create brand new business models that are able to correctly analyze the big data that have accumulated in the virtual environment with the internet, mobile applications and CBDs. Another huge advantage is that entrepreneurs no longer need to be programmers to be able to create a new Facebook or Angry Birds. As long as such an idea is interesting and worth attention, it is sufficient to follow digital clues using the basic ICTIQ skills of the entrepreneur. Therefore, whatever their sector or size may be, entrepreneurs should follow the trends in social media and the virtual environment closely. Again, in my opinion, investing especially in nature-friendly technologies in the short run will provide profitable opportunities for entrepreneurs.

Caution for your identity in the digital world while looking for jobs!

In the industrial society where the demands and desires of the individual were secondary, the priority of the individual was to have a profession that would bring in money. Instead of looking for the best job for ourselves, we were oriented towards jobs that would bring us money. It was out of the question to apply for jobs with a resumé in our parents' day. Whether we had a qualification or not, we were able to find a job with the help of our personal contacts, friends or relatives. For example, my father, who pursued his higher education in the 1950s, took classes from a few different universities simultaneously in the first few months of his education, and each of the three departments was a very different field of science: political science, dentistry and medicine. A few months later, he continued in the faculty of dentistry on the suggestion of a relative at the stage of his final decision, and became a dentist. In those years, as in the case of my father, our preference for a profession was determined by relatives and coincidences, or our teachers at high schools. Teachers were making recommendations by considering popular lines of work in the industrial society such as engineering, and providing suggestions. The process of having a profession and finding a job continued like this till about twenty-thirty years ago.

We received our university education this way till the first years of the Information Revolution, and made applications by sending our resumés to companies we wanted to work for. As we started to make the transition from the industrial society to the information society, we met new lines of work. Working dynamics in this process changed so rapidly that when a person enters university, the line of work they will work in after graduation is probably not invented yet.

In the past, if we could not find a job through our connections, we would use our contacts in the alumni association at our university. However, the platforms and groups provided by the internet made physical networking platforms obsolete. Our connections in the alumni associations may be useful, but we are now reaching them via e-mail lists or via WhatsApp. In summary, for employment, we have come to be using digital networks, namely Digital Ghettos that we are members of.

Rise of online employment platforms

A new business model was born for entrepreneurs after people started to find jobs by forming their Digital Ghettos and networks. Employment platforms like LinkedIn started to enter our lives. The data created within LinkedIn in the last few years were so valuable that Microsoft bought LinkedIn for four billion dollars. The most important quality that separates LinkedIn from other employment platforms is that you are able to see the relationships of all profiles in your network with other people. With the help of the detailed filtering feature in this platform, you are able to see the past career and personal characteristics of any person who has set up a profile. In summary, LinkedIn is not only an employment platform. After all, the monetary value of the information in its database is very high.

In addition to LinkedIn, which has become a global phenomenon, employment platforms that are designed for the working dynamics and needs of different countries have emerged in those countries. An example is Xing, which is an online employment platform widely used in Germany. In Germany, headhunters are more prevalent in comparison with human resources companies. Xing was developed by considering this situation. Instead of employing large numbers of people in the field of human resources, companies are looking for employees through limited research and the information provided, reached by keywords. Many search criteria on the system may also be reached through the mobile application. After registering for the system, you can apply for a job you find suitable by checking the daily notifications on the mobile application. In addition to this, there are dozens of platforms that target different lines of work and geographies.

Those who have ICTIQ have adapted to these developments on the field of employment easily and organized their job seeking processes on this basis. Effective usage of these platforms not only broadened the market (geography) in which they are looking for jobs, but it also helped the individual find the job that is the most suitable for the person's own professional knowledge and experiences.

> According to an article I recently read, professional connection platforms have now lost their purpose and started to be used as social media platforms. I do not know whether this will harm or support these platforms, but it will surely lead to an image change.

If your digital identity does not fit your real identity

According to some, messages shared in the digital world and social media and comments made are related to the personal life of the individual. Therefore it is not really fair to evaluate these in a way that will affect professional life. In fact, the opposite is the case in practice. While the social media posts and comments of an individual are related to their private life and personal views, serious problems may arise when organizations do not approve of these views that do not fit their own culture. Although we see expressions on social media like "these views are my own and not my employer's", it would be too optimistic to say these are taken seriously.

Another negative effect of employment platforms on employees or job seekers is Screen Addiction. I am sure that you also frequently encounter individuals who constantly check their phones in conferences that you attend for business purposes. While some create the impression that they are following their business, I do not need to tell you that they are busy with completely different things on their phones. Another group of professionals have an obsession with constantly following these platforms and learning about developments in the business world minute by minute. They even share some articles and sayings that they never read and whose content they never believed, with the purpose of establishing a reputation on these platforms. This kind of behavior reflects negatively on focusing on the job and productivity.

CBDs that create your emotional profile

While evaluating the professional identity of a candidate, many large companies today want to see the emotional profile of the person they are thinking of employing. While criteria such as adaptation to flexible working hours or graduation from certain schools were applicable in the industrial society, it was understood in time that these criteria are not sufficient for employment. As the importance of leadership skills, compatibility for teamwork, and skills in finding smart solutions is understood for an employer, the issue of creating an emotional profile increasingly gained significance.

As we mentioned in previous sections, Sensory Logic which makes it possible to read facial muscles and firms like I-motion, Noldus and Neuroinc that develop technologies that follow eye movements support companies who are in search of employees. This is how they determine whether the person is emotionally fit for the job or not.

New dynamics in employment

In short, as opposed to in the past, a person, especially in the first years of their professional life or career in the Information Society, is primarily looking for the job that is most suitable for themselves rather than the job the will bring in the most money. The case is similar for firms, too. Now they seek not the person with the most valuable diploma, but another who is the most suitable for the firm's culture and will provide the greatest support and contribution to the firm with their qualities. I think I do not even have to add how important ICTIQ is as a selection criterion.

In scope of our analyses, it may be argued that sending someone our resumé in the same sense as in the past has now become history. In addition to employment platforms like LinkedIn and Xing, new platforms that are suitable for the HR dynamics of different countries have emerged. The value of the data accumulated on these platforms has reached billions of dollars. Additionally, profiles are always open for access, mostly due to resumés that are kept online. In this case, classical networking that used to be limited to friends, family and acquaintances has been carried into the digital environment. A person that you are a complete stranger to but connected with through people you know is now able to easily reach your resumé via recommendations of internet applications or websites. Consequently, it is still possible to find a job through personal connections, but this field is now operated mostly through e-mail lists, social media groups and via platforms like WhatsApp.

While the Information Society provides advantages with the help of applications, it also presents a difficulty for people taking the first steps of their career due to its speed. This is because when the person starts university, the line of work they will work in will probably not have been invented yet. For example, people who are now working in a field such as Digital Content management probably did not receive training in this at university, because this line of work did not yet exist.

What is waiting for job seekers?

In addition to all these opportunities, it is another example of Digicrimination that people without ICTIQ cannot utilize new job-seeking methods, and some job applications can only be carried out online.

Moreover, jobseekers or people on online career platforms for any reason have started to obsessively follow whether a new position is open or not, or the career developments of their friends, acquaintances or even people they do not like. When this situation was combined with Screen Addiction, a mass that almost lived on these platforms emerged. On the other hand, people who are highly active on these platforms experience severe Digital Schizophrenia like that experienced on social media when their professional identity in the virtual environment does not fit their professional knowledge and experience.

It is a point worth noting that, while employing, firms are not only looking at our profile on the employment platform but they also monitor the posts we shared in the past in the virtual world. Additionally, employment criteria have started to include other measurement methods in addition to educational qualifications and work experience. Firms have started to conduct their interviews with not only classical personality tests and methods to read the body language but also software monitoring facial expressions and similar digital methods, and make a decision about the person who is applying for the job.

Reaching success while playing games

Do not ask "how could a person reach success while playing games, having fun, or 'fooling around' as old people would say." The concept of entertainment has changed so much with the Information Revolution that, now, playing games has become one of the musts of success, not just representing fooling around.

The accident experienced by a hardcore computer gamer friend of mine after being exposed to Digital Schizophrenia or similar examples should not create a negative perception that the lives of all regular players of digital games will be affected negatively. In fact, digital games provide us with a colorful world that increases a person's creativity, improves their competitive skills and opens the doors of strategic thinking. Therefore, there are significant differences between the generation who have grown up playing computer games and previous generations who have no experience of this sort in terms of their points of view about life. The Information Society youth who grew up with these games has more advantages of life success in comparison to older generations as they supported ICTIQ skills by other skills of fast and strategic thinking, competitiveness, risk taking and innovation. As these skills that they gained have become a part of their personality traits over time, it becomes easier for them to achieve success in both their personal and professional lives.

Individuals who are far from the world of digital games and entertainment, on the other hand, lose their competitive power over time, especially in the business world. I think we will soon witness more clearly the effects of Digicrimination which will be led in the professional field by young people who have been or will be trained with a tradition of playing digital games.

Indeed, if we look briefly at the historical data, we know that humankind has had the tradition of playing games / having fun since the earliest ages. We see in archeological excavations that people of the past produced toys that were inspired by the lifestyles of the communities they belonged to. For example, in the agricultural society, pagan societies placed stars at the top of pine trees when winter came and sunlight grew weaker; they organized celebrations to honor the return of spring and the sun, and played games during harvest festivities. This way, the concept of entertainment has continued to develop, sometimes through superstition / mystical beliefs and sometimes via religion. Each society developed games based on the geographical conditions and climate it experienced. This is why athleticism became popular in Africa while Austrians tended towards skiing.

According to some, games that are in the nature of humankind are also the basis of the sports-human relationship. Games are the first step towards the communication that a person establishes with their surroundings, starting with their baby steps and the basic behaviors that they need to learn to survive. Nevertheless, the famous scientist and founder of psychoanalysis Sigmund Freud, in his work titled *Beyond the Pleasure Principle,* talks about children developing behaviors through playing as they are not in control of what is happening around them. Humankind, which internalize many behaviors by itself or through a game taught by another, learns even the basic behaviors such as survival, reproduction, and satisfaction of the needs for food and shelter in this way. In other words, humankind learns about life through games.

Here, in order to reach a clearer picture, more detailed attention should be paid to *Les Jeux* by French sociologist Roger Callois. Callois carried Johan Huizinga's (and Umberto Eco's) view in *Homo Ludens* that "social culture" is supported, fed and developed by games into another dimension.[21]

By making another addition to the approach of Callois regarding the close relationship between culture and sports, it is possible to look at the relationship between sports and humans from different perspectives. In this context, while conceptually defining sports, one should mention the motivations that lie at its basis. In this context, it is possible to reflect on sports that behaviors occur in it such as creativity, pleasure, hate and aggressiveness that Sigmund Freud thought to be present in humankind by elaborating on the god of love, Eros, and the god of death, Thanatos. Winning and the satisfaction and pleasure of winning in sports are usually seen as the accepted motivations. However, defeating the competitor who is seen as the opponent and even seeing them defeated in another competition are sources of motivation and pleasure as much as the former. Although explanation of this factor is usually attempted through humor, it is certain that there are deeper reasons. It is actually possible to explain the existence of "hate speech" in today's sports in this context. In particular the approaches and attitudes of sports administrators such as "creating an enemy" and "showing the reason for failure" that are used frequently to cover their own conduct, manipulate facts and create a diversion, make this second type of motivation among the masses that follow sports more significant. Naturally, hate speech is nourished by this approach and gains power. As "hate speech" becomes more prevalent, sports and games are also affected by this.

---

21 Caillois, R. (1977). *Les jeux et les hommes: la masque et le vertige.* : Gallimard.
    Huizinga, J., & Eco, U. (2009). *Homo ludens.* Torino: Einaudi.

Factors that are emphasized by Callois in the game-sports relationship and the factors of motivation that we mentioned are definitely very important for an understanding of sports and stakeholders of sports today.

Sports as a social valve

Of course, development of the entertainment approach today is based on the period of the industrial society. While entertainment had been a concept that was cherished by the upper classes until that time, the concept of weekends emerged in order to prevent workers, who were the most important elements of the system of production, from rebelling against the conditions they were in. The working class, in order to relax and breathe a little, focused on entertainment at the weekends. Therefore, the popular entertainment culture was born around music, sports and food.

Another issue brought to us by the industrial society was the consciousness of identity. With the development of national, ethnic and even sexual identities, people's fields of conflict with each other were also diversified. People who fought for the lands they owned in the agricultural society started to fight in the name of the nation or ethnicity they were a part of. Development of such an area of conflict makes it more difficult to maintain the conflict on legitimate grounds.

Imagine that you are part of a minority that immigrated to a city for work. Imagine that you are exposed to constant discrimination in both your professional and personal life, and are trying to preserve your identity or rights. If you needed to be in constant conflict to protect yourself, your living conditions and responsibilities would not allow this. Therefore you have to establish the conflict on legitimate grounds. Indeed, sports competitions turn out to be life-saving in such cases. They not only carry the conflict and competition into a legitimate field, but also act as a social valve that releases anger through another channel. While one football team in a city represents the working class, another represents capitalist ideology. Ethnic groups support the team they feel close to themselves and continue their social conflicts through that team.

Sports competitions have opened up a significant area of competition not only in the local area, but also in the global arena. However, international dynamics have experienced a big change since the early 1990s after the collapse of the Berlin Wall and the end of the Cold War. The new national dynamics that emerged after the collapse of countries such as the Soviet Union or Yugoslavia led to creation of new teams. While, in many branches of sports, different techniques used to be adopted in communist and capitalist regimes, these techniques started to be intertwined and mixed. Athletes started to change countries and regimes, and ethnic identities started to be redefined.

A new industry is emerging

While ethnic identities and techniques were being redefined in the field of sports throughout the world, the Information Revolution took place during the same period. This way, we gained the opportunity to be able to follow sporting events in real time. The first dimension of real time was that we were now able to monitor the news about our favorite team minute by minute regardless of the distance. We achieved this sometimes via the internet online, or sometimes on television with the help of satellite broadcasts. The second dimension came when the concept of online betting came into our lives. With this development, a person in Germany became able to bet on a game played by a team in South Africa. Prominent sports branches throughout the world such as football have become fields that may be followed in real time by everyone and gather everyone's excitement by placing bets. We witnessed the rise of leading players whom we see as celebrities who have started to earn millions of dollars. All these changes turned sports into a world-wide industry. Even the personal lives of athletes are now products of this industry. While fans used to visit stadiums to compete against different ethnic identities in the past, they have now started to watch competitions with completely different motivations. Sports competitions have now become activities that are watched, enjoyed and quickly consumed, instead of events where conflict is experienced.

Prioritizing individualization

The possibility of watching sports events in real time and follow information about different games in different locations around the world simultaneously via social media has started to diminish the motivation to go to stadiums. People started to give up these habits after it became possible to watch sports on large screens and games with three-dimensional visuals and virtual reality. While sports events used to provide space for socializing, sports viewership has become an individual activity via these developments. Just like many elements in our lives, sports have also become a part of rapid consumption, and Digicrimination started to appear between the audiences that are able to watch events in real time and those that are not. In the light of these developments, it would not be wrong to argue that in ten years, sports seats will not be filled anymore and people will stop going to stadiums to watch games.

Sports and digital games intertwined

Computer games are now an industry in themselves. This field is usually in inter-section with the sports industry that has become huge through digitization. Video games of leading athletes are now very popular among the youth, and the new generation grows up playing these games. Even the establishment of such a habit is a significant event that led to changes in social dynamics. It is a phenomenon that changes society and the entertainment culture as we know it from scratch.

In fact, humankind has internalized and used games from the earliest periods of childhood. A baby that wants to get the attention of its mother tries to establish control over a certain situation by creating a game in its own way. Actually, eve-ryone who plays games simulates life by means of these games. The association of today's people with games is so deep that they are not satisfied by constant wins by the team they follow, but they also want the opposing team to lose.

While the Information Revolution supported a phenomenon that had such a place in our subconscious, the digital game industry has developed with incredible acceleration. With this synergy, the transference of games into mobile environ-ments and increases in the visual and auditory quality of technological devices have led people to dive increasingly deeper into the world of virtual games. It is no wonder that a phenomenon that affects human psychology so deeply creates Digital Schizophrenia. From a positive perspective, it is possible to argue that digital games will be an important factor in development in the following years. It is not possible for a child who has played simulation games and another who has not to achieve the same success in life.

Of course, the relationship between sports and the digital world is not limited to this. The image below that shows the relationship between sports events and related social media usage is the best example in current affairs. While games were being watched on TV, simultaneous social media shares were made. During the 2014 World Cup, 350 million people who commented on Facebook in relation to the event took part in 3 billion interactions. The most shares were from Brazil and the most talked-about athlete was Neymar. These numbers show us how habits of watching sports games have changed in such a short time.

More detailed statistics about this issue may be reached via the web page of Adweek on http://www.adweek.com/lostremote/infographic-world-cup-shatters-facebook-engagement-records/46217

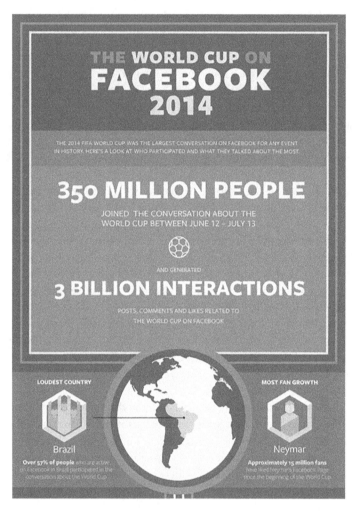

THE **WORLD CUP** ON
FACEBOOK
2014

THE 2014 FIFA WORLD CUP WAS THE LARGEST CONVERSATION ON FACEBOOK FOR ANY EVENT IN HISTORY. HERE'S A LOOK AT WHO PARTICIPATED AND WHAT THEY TALKED ABOUT THE MOST.

350 MILLION PEOPLE

JOINED THE CONVERSATION ABOUT THE
WORLD CUP BETWEEN JUNE 12 – JULY 13

AND GENERATED

3 BILLION INTERACTIONS

POSTS, COMMENTS AND LIKES RELATED TO
THE WORLD CUP ON FACEBOOK

LOUDEST COUNTRY

Brazil

Over 57% of people who are active on Facebook in Brazil participated in the conversation about the World Cup

MOST FAN GROWTH

Neymar

Approximately 15 million fans have liked Neymar's Facebook Page since the beginning of the World Cup

Statistics usage permitted by: Adweek

What changed in the world of sports?

First of all, in the clearest terms, sports became a world industry with the great contribution of online betting and video games that used star athletes. The influence of technology on viewing habits firstly took place through three-dimensional screens, and additionally, the visual nature of sports events developed, changed and became watchable by all kinds of means. Making sex objects out of athletes, and especially efforts to present female athletes in this way, is still a serious issue for debate.

The possibility of following sports competitions in real time with social media and other digital tools affected sports directly. Due to the Eros and Thanatos effect mentioned above, social media and sports achieve a great synergy. Just as people who calculate their food's image on social media while choosing it, an audience that follows sports competitions for the sake of their traces on social media rather than themselves was born. As this technological waywardness increased and it became easier to follow competitions from home, the habit of going to stadiums started to diminish, and accordingly, being a sports viewer became an individualized habit. Athletes became popular cultural icons and free global movement started. As a result of countries like China and Russia investing especially in football, the leagues of these countries started to gain attention and viewership.

Let us come to the part about digital games

The mind-boggling speed in technology, transition to the mobile environment and increases in the visual and auditory quality of game consoles naturally made the digital games market larger. This quality leads to such a realistic experience that people are assessing games as if they are simulations of life. The share of digital games in child development is undeniably high and young people who grow up with these are more successful in real life, but this also has a negative effect; shrinking of the difference between real life and digital game and the virtual and real approaching each other lead to Digital Schizophrenia. This will increasingly continue at a much faster speed with virtual and augmented reality.

I heard about the process regarding the criteria for the players chosen for the covers of the FIFA series, which was among the foremost games in the early 2000s, selection of music in the game and gathering similar components at first hand from one of the high-level executives of the firm, and while I was highly surprised, I also understood how important this industry is.

When food for the soul is digitized

Considering entertainment culture, the most important field which was the most heavily affected by the information revolution and caught off guard by technological developments is the music industry. Music products, in a gigantic industry involving musicians, record companies, concert halls and radios, used to travel to music markets and be consumed as vinyl records or cassettes. The first encounter of this field with digitization started with the transition from cassettes to CDs. Still, the prominent people in the industry, without whom the sector would be affected by digitized music, saw the CD as merely a new tool to bring music to the masses. In the same period, the prevalence of internet usage and emergence of the MP3 format which made it possible to store dozens or even hundreds of tracks on portable devices changed the music market from top to bottom. Up till then, music listeners were listening to music lists that they transferred from CDs to computers and continuing to use computers as CD players. This situation was changed forever by the initiation of the music-sharing platform named Napster. The thing that changed was not only the way we listened to music; an entire worldwide industry was shaken to its foundations.

The term *demassification* is now the best expression to describe the field of music as we know it today. In order to be able to understand this situation which we may summarize as stratification of music genres in terms of audiences and distribution of these to entire masses with diverse styles, it is enough to look at music portals that broadcast on the internet. For example, we now have access to music channels where we can find dozens of sub-genres within the genre that we previously called jazz as a blanket term.

With this development, audiences that previously bought media from music markets started to quit spending money on music products, and obtain copied products free of charge in the virtual environment. As in various other products in the digital environment, because there were no necessary legal regulations for music products in the digital environment, many prominent record companies, distributors, music markets and therefore musicians were dramatically affected by this development. By the time the necessary legislation was enacted about the copyright of music obtained from / listened to via the digital environment, the music industry was already and substantially harmed.

While the issue of copyright was redefined, many musicians found it extremely difficult to get used to the new distribution / consumption model. Most musicians were no longer able to earn money. In this period, Apple ran to the help of the sector and musicians. The software iTunes provided the possibility of buying music in a legal way in exchange for a price, even in mobile environments.

While a certain order was achieved in the sector with iTunes, buying and consuming music in the digital environment are still at the center of the debates. For example, the famous pop singer Taylor Swift, who complained that her royalties were not paid last year, sued Apple Music and declared that she was withdrawing some of her albums from the iTunes ecosystem. As music products were provided as albums in the past, they would arrive on the shelves with a significant price tag, and the consumer would pay attention when purchasing a CD. Still, the sales were not so impressive. With the start of shopping for music via digital music tracks, music consumption increased a lot and prices dropped. Like various products that we consume in the digital world, music has also become a part of fast-moving consumer goods. People are now buying music for very affordable prices and usually move to the next track without even finishing one. In summary, concepts like in-depth listening and being a good listener to music are on the brink of becoming history.

Such fast consumption of music has led musicians and the world of music to become shallower. Today, a new musician makes a debut every minute and every day, but they do not last due to this shallowness; pieces of music and melodies do not feed our souls. There are so many songs shared through social media, YouTube and different digital channels that it is extremely difficult to distinguish qualified musicians in this cacophony. Within this movement of fast consumption, singing and talent competitions have become popular all around the world. While we may sometimes see people with high-quality voices among participants who want to showcase themselves in these competitions, viewers are watching these to listen to the personal success story of the participant rather than for the quality of the music presented. This approach continues to eviscerate music and this environment of chaos that the musicians are in is not adequate for new talents to shine. Stars like Michael Jackson and Madonna are no longer emerging.

Popular music has always been easier to consume. Nevertheless, I think the duration of this consumption is shorter than ever today. I believe the main factors here are works that are easily uploaded on digital platforms especially YouTube and listened to for free. On the other hand, when there is the example of Justin Bieber, who owes his high fame and glory to his mother who shared his amateur recordings on YouTube, it would be meaningless to claim the opposite.

On the other hand, ironically, it is a matter of time before musicians who cannot use social media effectively fall out of favor, regardless of how good they are. Today's pop stars such as Adele are able to protect their popularity by using social media actively and managing the ecosystem better. Musicians and bands that became famous in the past are trying to protect their popularity by creating different publicities, like the famous band U2 taking on the field of humanitarian aid and supporting such activities... On the other hand, the worldwide popularization of digital games has also created a new area of competition for musicians. While game companies used to run after musicians for background music to use in their games in the past, today musicians are running after game companies for collaboration.[22]

Journey of music in digital

To cut a long story short, it is evident that the most dramatic change in the entertainment sector was experienced in the music industry. When music became easily obtainable and quickly consumable, its fundamental axis experienced a substantial shift. The music industry increased in volume several times. The possibility of listening to it on mobile devices everywhere and upload hundreds of tracks on mobile phones made it possible to listen to music at any time of day. The music industry continued to grow through Napster and similar applications which enforcements were insufficient to prevent, but many musicians, producers and studios found themselves in a place where they could no longer earn money. Additionally, legal music downloading applications such as iTunes acted as a lifeline by bringing the process of copyright into the digital environment.

There are undeniably popular views that these developments in the world of music and fast consumption of music on social media prevent the production of high-quality music. I agree. Additionally, copyright still poses a problem. Trying to guarantee copyright by old methods also fails.

Being popular in the world of music now has its own rules and dynamics. Musicians who manage social media wall stay in the spotlight and increase their brand value. On the other hand, musicians who became popular earlier but are now finding it difficult to adjust to the new times, including Madonna, are in search of new methods to stay in the limelight. They are occasionally trying to stay in the front line with polemics, sensational news, and made-up scandals. Talent competitions and the chaos in the virtual world also make it difficult for good musicians to shine and be heard. If you look at the global music market today, you may see how effective the talent competition The Voice or shows like the Victoria's Secret new year show are in consumption in the world. Although the Voice in particular is a vocal talent competition, the ratings of the competitors are not based on their talent, but depend on their personal stories. Audiences who sob intensely are blended with entertaining jury members to promote skills of acting and showmanship instead of talent. The interesting part is that no competitor who competed in this show successfully or even came first has found a significant place for themself in the music market.

---

22 How To Get Your Music Into Video Games. (n.d.). Retrieved in 2017, from http://www.hypebot.com/hypebot/2011/04/advice-getting-your-music-into-video-games-.html.

It would be unfair to say that there are no developments supporting the world of music. The sports, gaming, entertainment and cinema sectors support the music market in different ways. Although the roles have changed and musicians came to be pursuing digital game companies to get their music featured, the contributions of these fields to music cannot be ignored.

Digital passwords and the new concept of security

As one of the instinctive motivations of a person is survival, the need for security becomes one of the basic needs. Humankind in early ages took shelter in order to achieve physical security, and then built its own shelters later. In terms of evolution, while humans gained an advantage over other species by climbing to the top of the food chain, our need for security has never ended. However developed the history of humanity may be, the issue of security has always been among the top problems that need to be solved.

When we reached the agricultural society, the need to protect ourselves and our families in a physical sense was joined by the need to protect our land, house and belongings. As people were achieving production from the soil, received their food from it and made a living this way, they surrounded agricultural land with fences, and when necessary, they fought to protect their land and keep their living space.

With social development, people gained an identity and a social role. Therefore, another issue that needed to be secured emerged: the identity and social status one had. This time, security within society was added to physical security. When the transition to social life as we know it today started, people understood that they needed to protect themselves against other people. As in the famous expression *homo homini lupus,* meaning "man is wolf to man", rules and established legal systems naturally emerged and laws were made to protect and guarantee the set of basic rights one possesses. These were regulated by the legitimate power of states. It was accepted that if illegality became legitimate in the society, huge chaos was inevitable.

In this case, the concept of security did not remain individualistic, but also became the most significant agenda of states. Security measures were taken to protect the lands, fields and trade areas. In the industrial society, beyond the security of the materials in one's own soil, another issue emerged to protect the raw materials that would sustain one's industry and energy infrastructure. This new need led to the start of colonialism, which is the root of some social and economic problems that are still ongoing today. The origins of colonialism carry the traces of countries such as the United Kingdom that pioneered the industrial revolution. Countries which could not obtain oil which was of critical significance for industry in their own lands chose the way of taking control of other people's lands. This action triggered world wars, and several countries in the world, whether their industry was advanced or not, made military investments and developed strategies to secure themselves against this new threat.

The definition of security is changing

During the industrial society, the definition of security remained physical, regardless of individual or state issues. However, the definition of security also changed with the Information Revolution. When critical data about individuals and states started to be transferred to the virtual world, we encountered a new phenomenon in protection and security of these data. Digital passwords that we needed in many fields from internet banking to our e-mail addresses became the most important elements of our information security.

Without being limited to the protection of personal and corporate information, digital security started to have critical importance for the functioning of essential systems and sectors. Everything, including but not limited to electricity and urban transportation, was moved from analog systems to digital systems for easier management. There were two ways to destroy such infrastructures: physically damaging the system or disabling it from a different location on earth using a virus or similar software. While they were not initially taken very seriously, early Information Revolution period hackers like Kevin Mitnick showed what kinds of damage will result to such an infrastructure when it is made dysfunctional. The damage made to any system via software would create damage that is almost equivalent to the damage that would be caused by a bomb. This is how the definition of digital security came to be known to everyone.

It was understood that not only companies or large infrastructure systems but also strategic data and facilities of countries were also facing a security threat. For example, if you disabled the systems of a country for an hour with the help of a virus that would penetrate its electricity infrastructure, this would create costs for that country that would go far beyond a day's damage to the economy. This situation that was not taken seriously and even belittled is now a reality of life.

Legal experts experienced serious issues in the early period of the Information Revolution as the necessary regulations and legal infrastructure about digital security threats did not yet exist. Many cyber-crimes in countries without legislation about informatics had to be evaluated on the basis of penal codes for years. Judges who had never used a computer in their entire lives had to make decisions about something that they knew nothing about. Today, even if a theft takes place in the digital environment, it is evaluated as a cyber-crime. Countries which have not yet created legal regulations about cyber-crimes are still experiencing issues about this subject. Digital security has become a primary issue that needs to be taken seriously and given attention all around the world. Brand-new IT companies have been established to achieve digital security, and they have started to market products focusing on the security threats in question.

There were many agenda items in 2016 about the American elections that concerned the whole world, but I think the most important ones were the usage of a personal e-mail address for correspondence by the candidate Hillary Clinton, and the claims that Russian hackers influenced the vote counts by interfering with the elections. If we had written the sentence more than twenty years ago, besides being surreal, it would sound ridiculous. These are still huge mysteries for a large part of the public, but they are now part of the reality of our lives.

New security issues brought about by social media

When cyber-crimes targeted large organizations in earlier times, we started to encounter a new security issue in the digital environment with the prevalence of social media. People experienced the problems of having shared their personal or private information, especially in the first stages of social media. Books, projects and personal photos transferred to the digital environment may lead to problems regarding copyright. People's social media passwords are now as important as the passwords of their physical safes. Besides, removal or elimination of any information once it has been distributed on the internet is another problem in itself. The number of companies providing services for removal of digital footprints is not very low.

As any process in our lives is based on our ICTIQ knowledge and digital literacy in the Information Society, older generations that are not qualified in this matter may be exploited and conned via their mobile phones or computers which they find difficult to use. At this point, a large audience that is exposed to Digicrimination is at the center of discrimination.

While the concept of security shifts from hardware to software, the environments in which we store our data and how alert and informed we are about these environments carry importance.

From physical security to digital passwords

In summary, the changing ecosystem of the Information Society brought new concepts into our lives, and the concept of physical and psychological security that was carried into the digital environment with the Information Revolution is one of these.

Transfer of personal information into a virtual environment and management of infrastructures like electricity distribution and banking brought us face to face with a new security threat. While warnings were issued that attacks using virus software have an impact power like those of physical bombs, the gravity of the issue was understood only after experiencing it. Hackers became a part of our lives. In fact, they became an inseparable part. New security companies whose field of operation is different to those of conventional security companies were established. Older people who did not have ICTIQ skills or information literacy were subjected to Digicrimination in this sense. Hence, of course, the passwords of social media accounts that became central to privacy became more important than the passwords of physical safes.

Interestingly, companies that provide services that make removal of posts that are regretted later and personal information that is spread in the virtual environment took their place among the lines of work that emerged with the Age of Information.

Transition to global governance through digital campaigns

The world has gradually become globalized due to increased usage of the internet for both personal and commercial purposes and development of social media and telecommunications. As geographical distances were now meaningless after the emergence of the virtual environment, we started to learn about events and developments that happened on the other side of the world in an instant. Societies that used to be strangers to each other got closer in time, and in addition to receiving news about an event in other locations, societies started to be influenced by developments. While there are still geographical borders and traditional state structures today, we have started to show awareness and claim rights regarding historical and environmental values that are accepted as cultural heritage. These developments gave rise to the concept of world citizenship.

Even a person who is living on the opposite side of the world is concerned about the archeological sites that are ruined during wars in the Middle East. Even if they are not geographically close, they try to take action to protect the cultural heritage. This awareness and need to take action have led to increased usage of platforms such as Change.org where digital petition campaigns are organized. We have come to have a say in developments on the other side of the world with the help of such digital platforms.

While people used to organize protests about governments through local newspapers and mass communication tools in the past, it is now possible to start campaigns on social media, spread them, make ourselves heard about a subject, raise awareness and achieve change. Thus a global and digital movement in the field of governance has started. Social media is now a new factor of pressure in governance that cannot be ignored.

People who are not following social media closely today are exposed to serious discrimination regarding direct participation in government. The new concept of governance that emerged on digital platforms has actually opened a new window for subjects that are crucial, such as democracy and direct participation in government. In many countries today, political elections are held via computers. While electronic voting provides easy operation, voting via electronic environments is extremely prone to rigging. Manipulation of information transferred to a digital environment is much easier than any intervention in the physical environment. This situation shows that there is a need for development of new formulas to encourage people who are used to the old method to go to the ballot box. One of the biggest problems of our time is people's loss of belief in democracy. Loss of belief in democracy increasingly curbs the number of potential voters who actually vote. The Brexit vote, the decision for war in the referendum in Colombia that asked for a decision between "war and peace" and the referendum result in Hungary that prevented only 1,300 refugees from entering the country are the most recent indications of this disbelief.

New concepts that need to be discussed by scientists

On the other hand, it is really hard to predict what effect a post will create on social media. While an important issue such as torture inflicted on animals in zoos does not sometimes get enough attention, let us say, a campaign to save a historical restaurant that will be affected by construction in Tokyo may create a huge reaction. The key point there is the correct presentation of the idea about which awareness is to be raised. Yet understanding why subjects like eliminating poverty or saving a large cedar-wood forest from annihilation do not always get attention is a subject that needs to be focused on by scientists, especially psychologists. Additionally, political scientists and law practitioners also have important roles in understanding the developments in governance and making necessary modifications.

Political scientists, like social scientists, still generally prefer to talk about how liberal and realist movements are affecting each other. A few years ago, I asked a friend of mine who is a professor of law the following: "There are studies that are planning to transfer the information on the human brain to a memory card in the near future. There is even a project called 2045 Initiative that works on this.[23] Then,

---

23 The Project can be followed on www.2045.com.

when I transfer the information in my mind to a virtual environment, who will have the intellectual ownership of this information? The public or my family? Is this information, as it is information that affects the public, going to be considered as a cultural entity? Should it be collected within an institution?"

My friend did not answer any of the questions. He told me that he would study this issue and avoided answering my questions. Such issues may seem to be utopian, fantastic issues for law scholars and academics. However, people in technology are continuing to work on these. Considering the speed of technology, the thing I am talking about might happen even before 2045. However, it is not too hard to guess that legal experts will fall behind on this issue, just as they were behind with regulations about self-driving cars… The law is, unfortunately, always late in reacting. When the fundamental fields that affect the relationships in society fall behind, these factors affect Digicrimination positively. As politics and law are fields that affect the direction in which society is moving, scientists should show more effort on these issues.

Political scientists, on the other hand, are expecting a much more serious and deeper agenda in the near future. For example, beyond their status as cultural heritage, let us discuss the massacre of the Amazon forests that are the lungs of our world. Is the Brazilian government the only party responsible for activities such as forestry and mining in this region? Should the decisions about the Amazon forests be taken by local authorities or citizens of the world? Again, if I am voting in the digital environment about the restoration of the church of Notre Dame in Paris, which is accepted as a piece of world heritage, and can have a say about the modifications, will I not have a right to vote in the Parisian municipal elections? If digital voters are as responsible as Parisians, do they not have a right to vote on some issues? Or should they?

Virtual citizenship is coming

Apart from the subjects that need to be discussed by legal experts and political scientists, states will start in the near future to provide new implementations concerning virtual citizenship. As you know, when you are born, you enter a contract with the state of the country that you are accepted as a citizen of. What you call the state is a legitimate power to which you transfer some of your rights as agreed. With this contract, you are saying to the state: "Protect me from external powers". In exchange for this service, you are agreeing to give a certain amount of taxes to the state, and promise to abide by the rules set forth by that state. There is an implicit, agreed contract between you and the state. By birth, without the right to choose, you became a citizen of some country based on religion, language, ethnicity or geography. Additionally, you are working as a member in the economy of that country. It may also be stated that, in the industrial society, in order to prevent inquiry about this situation, countries were established on the basis of a set of elements of attachment such as nation, religion, ideology and ethnic background.

As economic relationships have changed and become globalized in the new world order, some changes need to take place in this contract between the citizen and the state. The citizen who produces and pays taxes votes for politicians in exchange for the services received. For the person who made the contract, there are both the responsibilities and rights of the citizen within the jurisdiction of that country. If we carry these rights and responsibilities into digital form, whether or not you have visited a country or are living in that country, it becomes possible for you to be considered a citizen of that country. We are now already seeing similar examples. For example, if you invested to buy a house in Spain, Portugal or Greece, you gain the right to reside in that country within a certain procedure. By just having spent a certain amount of time in that country in a year, it is sufficient for you to become a type of "virtual" citizen. This way, you also gain the right to vote online. After a period, anyone with money may gain the citizenship of a country that they have never visited.

While these practices are becoming increasingly prevalent, I think the practice of virtual citizenship will enter our lives in some form in the near future. Just like the USA providing Green Cards for people via a lottery today, we may expect that virtual citizenship will also take place in exchange for a price. As the concept of nation-states is still valid today, it might not be possible for virtual citizens to have all the rights enjoyed by the regular citizens of that country. However, various countries with decreasing populations or increasing average age may provide such an opportunity for citizens of other countries, especially with the aim of utilizing labor. Maybe a European country would prefer to take on this practice for foreigners who are over a certain IQ level and experts in a line of work. Separate passports may be created for virtual citizens.

Some time ago, a man formed his own state in the small territories between Croatia and Hungary. Many people gave him money to become citizens of that state. You may have read this as a clownish tabloid article, but considering the new trends about citizenship, this practice was very real and meaningful.

It may sound eccentric, but we were recently introduced to the concept of space citizenship. A call was made last year for a space nation named Asgardia to be established. In a short time, more than 470 thousand people had already applied for citizenship of Asgardia, designed as a satellite-country to be launched into space. This may seem utopian, but what we are talking about today was utopic just twenty years ago. The old concept of a new world appears to be becoming real. [24]

Apparently, in the near future, we will encounter designs such as space citizenship, virtual citizenship and similar applications more frequently. The relationship between the state and the citizens will get softer and change with such implementations. It should not be a surprise if this subject is opened for debate in the United Nations.

In summary

We started to live in a globalized world with the Information Revolution and prevalent usage of the internet. In addition to many other concepts, globalization brought the concept of world citizenship into our lives. Today, people can claim rights over regions, monuments and geographies that are considered as the world's cultural heritage as there is now more awareness of them and feelings about such issues can now be transmitted to large audiences through shares.

As opposed to the past, it is now easier to get organized for such shout-outs. With the help of online campaigning platforms on the internet such as Change.org and social media, individuals are now interfering with practices of companies or countries and having a say in the decision-making mechanism. There is now a serious debate on whether world citizens should have a say in the management of world heritage regions such as the Amazon forests which are the lungs of the world. In this case, obviously, we are facing several problems that need to be solved by experts in law and politics.

On the other hand, the definition of citizenship has become different due to differentiation, softening and flexibility of the definition of nation-states. For example, countries with economic problems have already started to give residence permits to those who invest or buy houses in their country. It would not be wrong to argue that countries with ageing populations or those who need labor will soon start to sell virtual citizenship.

---

24 https://asgardia.space/en/.

Social media that articulates feelings

The latest trick of the Information Revolution has become the change that it created in people's lives through social media. Maybe because social media appeals to the most basic emotions of people, it became a phenomenon in our daily lives. It did not only affect our way of behavior; it is also playing a leading role as a tool of organization in mobilizing the masses. Various fields, from marketing to politics, are still changing and transforming with the effects of social media. While achieving this transformation, social media are progressing by touching all components of Digicrimination from Screen Addiction to Digital Schizophrenia.

Defense, adoption, learning and connection

Well, where does social media get this power from? The answer is actually simple. It refers to our instincts and basic emotions directly. Additionally, according to a study conducted at Harvard University, the human brain releases dopamine, known as the happiness hormone, while using social media.[25] Behavior-wise, people act by a set of motivations while taking any action. The top motivation among these is the instinct of defense that they show with the aim of protecting themselves, their status and what they have, and thus through fear. We want to protect our ideals and certain values that we have or we believe we have. The possibility of losing these values of ours creates fear in us. Sharing is one of the best ways of overcoming fear. People share what they have on social media by developing a defense mechanism, and try to get rid of a basic fear.

On the other hand, we see and like many products and services that we appreciate through social media. When we see on social media that there is a new smartphone in the market, that smartphone becomes our new target. That is, social media immediately trigger our motive to adopt.

One of the important advantages given to us by social media is learning. We become informed about events around the world in real time, and learn about developments in an instant. Before news agencies, or cable services write about a news story and send it to news organizations and the public, we have the chance to learn about it on social media. Besides, while media organizations occasionally provide partial news and try to manipulate the reader, we have the chance to look at a video shot and shared at the time of the event by a citizen, and see

---

25 Tamir, D.I.&Mitchell, J.P.(2012). Disclosing information about the self is intrinsically rewarding.Proceedings of the National Academy of Sciences. 109 (21), 8038–8043. Doi:10.1073/pnas.1202129109.

the raw version of the news that is not interpreted or doctored. This interactive environment of social media has taught people not only to use multimedia effectively, but also to express developments in a short and concise way using one hundred and forty characters. In global mass movements such as the Arab Spring, it turned into a platform where we could follow events through the eyes and ears of the locals instead of official bodies. This usage characteristic of social media played an important role in organization and accurate information of the public.

Likewise, social media also provided a new ground for socialization, one of the biggest needs of humankind. We reconnected with old friends we had not been in contact with for a long time in the busy flow of life by communicating with them via social media. Even though we cannot take part in the lives of our loved ones living in distant geographies in a physical way, we know that they are alive through the photos and videos they share on Facebook. In the past, people would go to alumni reunions to get together with their old friends. Social media are now filling this gap.

Therefore, people immediately embraced social media, which mobilized their acts of defense, adoption, learning and connection knowingly or unknowingly, and accepted them into their lives. We cannot even think about a life without social media anymore. However, older generations who cannot become active on this platform, and those who are deprived of social media, stay uninformed about developments around them to a great extent, and become exposed to discrimination.

Meeting point for exhibitionists and voyeurs

One should not forget that social media, which pioneer various positive developments by appealing to people's emotions and instincts, also have some negative effects on society and the individual due to the same characteristic. Social media, which contribute to our improvement in issues such as sharing and learning, improve us on the one hand, while revealing our dark sides on the other. One of these negative effects is the issue of voyeurism. Social media have a structure that triggers this type of behavior that was studied in depth by people such as Foucault and Lacan, and the science of psychology. While people continued the process of alienation through the virtual, idealized profiles they create on social media, on the other hand, they also developed a tendency to constantly monitor and stalk the profiles of people they are in contact with on social networks, so that, this behavioral disorder has taken an obsessive form for some people. By the mixture of real and virtual lives into each other, a significant confusion started to appear in the perceptions of people. Many people, knowingly or unknowingly, are using social networks to gain attention. As in the real world, people desire that what they are saying will be listened to and they will be found funny on social platforms. Therefore they prefer to share posts on social networks to imply the meaning "I look at things differently". On some topics, we all witness people who try to get attention by sharing the exact opposite of the idea they actually believe in. Moreover, vulgar/negative shares usually get more followers on social media. Millions of people with attitudes of "no such thing as bad publicity" share posts on social networks with heart and soul with the aim of reaching more people than others do, getting followers, gaining approval, shining out, becoming famous, or, in other words, satisfying their ego.

• *Concepts like exhibitionism, voyeurism, control mechanisms, surveillance mechanisms of power have been discussed by various philosophers and thinkers. Naturally, works by thinkers such as Jeremy Bentham and Michel Foucault that start with the panopticon structure are those that need to be read by people who are interested in this subject. George Orwell's 1984 is also a must to follow.*[26]

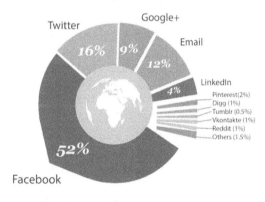

Statistics usage permitted by: Login Radius https://2yu5yy2vwpsr4dg1ys3jha9o-wpengine. netdna-ssl.com/wp-content/uploads/2016/04/2016_Q1_Social-Sharing-Global-Popularity.png

The chart above compares the volumes of platforms used for content sharing in 2016. While the numbers may change in time, there are no big differences in ratios.

---

26 Orwell, G. (2016). *1984*. Lexington, KY: Publisher not identified.

On this platform, exhibitionism stands right across voyeurism. Many people who want to stand out are not even aware of how much of their private lives they are sharing with masses in an uncontrolled manner while they are sharing their photos and videos. Many social media users have still not understood that a selfie is a kind of exhibitionism. By all these reasons, the most important reason for this popularity of social media is a structure that allows voyeurism and exhibitionism. When this structure is combined with different addictions of ours like Screen Addiction, it takes a form that affects human psychology deeply.

Social media of the future

Tendencies show that social media will take a very different form in the next few years. Just as Microsoft became highly popular with the new Windows operating system in the first years of PCs and then started losing popularity, we might expect that there will be a similar transformation in social networks. In the following years, social media will evolve into a very different state, for example, when they make it possible to make direct purchases. On the other hand, whichever shape social media might have in the future, it is a fact that it holds a significant behavioral dataset about people on the virtual environment. Even today, Facebook monitors our tendencies by tracking the websites we visit, and when we visit social media again, it brings advertisements and pages that are related to the subjects we are interested in. While this practice is scary, it is an inevitable phenomenon. Second by second, firms that manage social networks monitor and record which photos we liked, which videos we watched, which games we played and which news stories we read. It would be naïve to expect that a platform that accumulates such large amounts of data will not be used for commercial purposes.

If we want to protect our personal security and private life, we need to be very careful about what we are sharing.

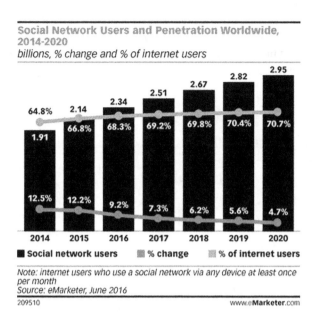

Social Network Users and Penetration Worldwide, 2014-2020
billions, % change and % of internet users

Note: internet users who use a social network via any device at least once per month
Source: eMarketer, June 2016

209510

www.eMarketer.com

Statistics usage permitted by: E-marketer
https://www.emarketer.com/Chart/Social-Network-Users-Penetration-Worldwide-2014-2020-billions-change-of-internet-users/190584

The chart above summarizes social media usage in the period 2014–2020 in contrast to internet usage. This chart is important as it shows that social media usage will increasingly continue in the following years.

In summary: What did the inevitable rise of social media change?

As it appears, social media have become such a large phenomenon as they mobilize people's motives to defend, adopt, learn and connect, and appeal to their most basic emotions and instincts. Social media also contribute to our lives positively with their possibilities, such as receiving the news in real time and getting organized in emergencies. Voyeurs who are obsessed with following others' lives and exhibitionists who love selfies obviously found what they were looking for on social media. One could argue that social media trigger Screen Addiction and Digital Schizophrenia. Furthermore, the big data on social media continue to grow in a way that whets the appetites of firms, countries and even intelligence agencies. Analysis of these big data and the behavior data accumulated on social media show that in the future, social networks will go beyond merely being larger shopping platforms.

Section 4. Values and relationships are being redefined

The Information Revolution not only transformed the traditional working fields of the industrial society, but it also influenced our relationships and ways of communication from the foundations. Our communication has been influenced by technological developments across history, but with this revolution for the first time, the modality, namely the nature of communication, has changed from scratch. As communication forms the essence of interaction among people, our individual relationships have taken a very different turn.

As the structures that form the founding stones of life changed, human relationships that are dependent on these also started to be transformed. Different generations have different ways of communication now. It is as if they are broadcasting in different frequencies. As one of the parties in the relationship moved to a different modality, even if the concepts it defines in its life are the same for the other party in terms of names, they carry different meanings in terms of expression. The meanings of concepts such as friendship, companionship, family ties and life success are completely different for the two generations. Therefore, even if they are in dialogue while they are communicating, it becomes increasingly difficult for them to understand each other. Regardless of age differences, this incompatibility between generations is experienced by everyone today, between those who use social media, have ICTIQ or play computer games, and those who do not. This is why we need to look at our way of communication, how relationships are established in the Age of Information, and accordingly, how our values are differentiated. It is obvious that the concepts in question should be redefined.

A new sub-culture emerging on the internet

Following the widespread usage of the internet, several people in different parts of the world started to communicate with each other. This way, we witnessed the emergence of new platforms for telecommunication. The first bases that were born for communication on the internet were e-mail lists and websites with forums on them. Groups of people gathered around a subject created their small e-mail lists and started communicating. Forums referred to wider audiences. With the help of forums, we gained the chance to communicate with people who were from different parts of the world but with whom we were able to gather around a subject. These platforms led to separation of groups that used to communicate

117

in the physical environment in the past. For instance, some of the members of a group that established a foundation to organize group activities about the environment and had carried out meetings for decades started to gather on these forums on the internet and interact via these platforms. Naturally, the foundation members who were not participants in these e-mail lists or forums felt excluded all of a sudden. They missed the agenda discussed in the virtual environment, and remained uninformed about some meetings. Thus they experienced the first effects of Digicrimination.

In the first periods of forums, namely the late 1990s, users found themselves in a free environment without any rules. Digital Schizophrenia started to show itself with the use of nicknames, and people had started to treat each other with a different psychology in an environment that was independent from real life. When there came an issue of organization about a subject, they could take on a much more militant attitude than in real life. This trend led to the language to be much braver and more daring. Those who had better writing and literature skills assumed leadership on the forums. These people, whom we may call keyboard warriors, were followed intensively. When the need for managing digital communities came up, the position of an admin was born. Forums became increasingly abundant and diverse. While Volkswagen owners would create a group or a forum at first, after some time, smaller groups started to be formed for Volkswagen Passat or Tiguan users.

As information technology law had not developed in this period, people were able to write about and share things that were illegal or had criminal sanctions in the forums. People were even able to sell tickets on the black market via these forums. In time, these environments were subjected to some regulations. However, the language of communication that was formed in that period is still going on. As people do not come face to face with people they are communicating with and as they are in a virtual environment, they may use words that they would never say in real life.

Nevertheless, despite all this looseness and disorderliness, forums provided us with an incredible treasure: free sharing of information. We became able to access information that we previously could not, thanks to these platforms. We were able to ask questions about a certain subject of an expert living on the other side of the world, and to receive answers. Forums that turned into a sub-culture in time are still continuing to develop. Forums, just like social media or newspapers, turned into tools for distributing news. Today, for example, we can easily read about views on the quality of the service provided by a hotel on that hotel's website. In fact, these views/reviews are gifts to us from the forum culture that previously developed. In the virtual environment of today, almost no one takes the position of not answering a question directed towards them. There is almost a contract of chivalry among masses that have understood the value of sharing information. Today, each forum has developed a culture and discourse unique to itself. It is possible to visit any forum and have an idea about that forum's culture through discourse analysis.

Looking for true love in a virtual environment

Considering the general outlook of the history of humanity, it would not be wrong to argue that the Digital Revolution effected a change in relationships very fast. The change happened so fast and swiftly. Despite this, people adopted the new relationship dynamics in a short time. Although romantic relationships are now being exhausted faster, free expression of expectations towards the nature of relationships has gained the approval of society. Romantic relationships aside, subjects such as sex, eroticism and pornography that are related to sexuality stopped being taboo subjects with the internet. The possibility of access to websites by everyone changed our moral values and led to a transformation in the understanding of romantic relationships.

When the new platform of communication and socializing was the internet, romantic relationships were also carried into the virtual environment. Nevertheless, the virtual nature of the environment does not mean that you cannot find true love here. One of the biggest needs of humanity involves finding a suitable partner, having a family, procreation and continuing one's bloodline. Being bonded by marriage or having children is also an indicator of social status. The institution of marriage is indispensable for traditional patriarchal societies. Actually, the dynamics of the institution of marriage and romantic relationships started to change with the industrial society. While special activities, dances and festivals were organized for marrying men and women at first, after awareness about women's rights started to develop, women achieved the freedom to choose the people they would marry. Women's involvement in labor during WWII and later and their access to economic power also affected marriage. When economic difficulties started to appear in this period, people's life concerns, personal preferences and priorities became more important than establishing a family. Cases of divorce became more prevalent day by day, and many people preferred to live alone or bring up children by themselves rather than marrying.

Individual economic freedoms of men and women led them to be reluctant about sharing the money that they earned with much difficulty. This is how the traditional idea of establishing a family and romantic relationships became different. Dates that used to be held secretly in the past later became easier and started to gain approval from society. Still, people's motives such as experiencing love, having sex and socializing did not disappear. With digitalization, the place where people seek romantic love became the virtual world.

Dating sites that replaced letters

After watching the movie *You've Got Mail,* shot in the late 1990s, namely the first periods of the Information Revolution, and starring Tom Hanks and Meg Ryan, we all believed that we could have a romantic relationship via the internet. This movie, which depicted a connection with a mysterious partner that we cannot meet face to face, was portraying romantic relationships that were being transferred into the digital world, yet in a naïve way in comparison to today. In fact, before the phenomenon of digitization shook the world, romantic relationships had already started to lose their romance.

In time, many people started to flirt over the internet, just like in the movie *You've Got Mail,* find a relationship, experience love and find sexual partners. Institutionalization of this development in the virtual world was pioneered by dating sites. These sites brought an analytical dimension to partner selection by completely removing the element of mystery. Individuals started to set up profiles on dating sites and communicate with people who had similar traits or attracted their interest. Various applications were developed for dating with the prevalence of mobility. These platforms specialized among themselves and formed structures that appealed to certain geographies, ethnic or religious backgrounds.

Relationships were taken onto a more materialistic level with all these developments. The nature of romantic relationships is now moving in the opposite direction to what romantic relationships meant previously. People who used to write romantic love letters to know about the person they liked in the past are now browsing the profiles on dating websites to find a suitable partner for themselves. Individuals originally used to join their lives with people to whom they felt close and for whom they had romantic emotions, and then try to know them and learn about their personal traits. On today's dating sites, they start first to try to learn and know about their personality traits. They started to follow a tendency to examine the profile they noticed, and to establish a romantic relationship by starting with information about the person's career, likes and hobbies. The old order is now reversed.

If we look at the predictions about the incomes of dating sites, my comment would be that there is an increase in this area but this increase is not progressing so fast.

Questions multiplying with values turning upside down

Considering the general outlook of the history of humanity, it would not be wrong to argue that the Digital Revolution effected a change in relationships very fast. The change happened so fast and swiftly. Despite this, people adopted the new relationship dynamics in a short time. With the communication modality that is brought by digitization, our value judgments and moral points of view have changed radically in comparison to the ways of our relationships in the industrial society. Adoption of casual language while communicating in the virtual world destroyed the etiquette that is expected in the physical environment. When we go to a doctor's appointment or attend a meeting in a new location, we use titles and formal language to address the people in front of us. However, we can now easily address people that we do not know at all, those whom we have never met, on a first-name basis and using informal language on the internet. Whenever we are not face to face with people we are talking to, our way of addressing them changes immediately. We do not even think about whether the language we are using fits good manners.

Besides, in this virtual environment without eye contact, we now have a tendency to easily steal a piece of information that belongs to another person. A short time ago, I shared a photo that I had previously shot and edited on social media for commemorative purposes. In a short time, I noticed that a friend of mine shared the same image, adding another comment. When I asked why they did not ask for my permission before using the image, the answer was "did you also not use someone else's image?". This dialogue led me to think about how comfortable we are while using a piece of information that belongs to someone else in the virtual environment. While the essence of the issue is plagiarism, the following questions immediately arise:

– Does a piece of information or a visual I have shared on social media belong solely to me?
– Do others have to get my permission while using my content?
– If I think permission is required and my friend does not, in other words, if we do not behave on the basis of the same value judgments, how should my relationship with my friend continue?

These questions lead to different questions regarding the manner of communication that takes place on social media or any platform in the virtual environment. Can we share a photograph we took with a friend in the virtual world in any way without getting their permission? Are we violating their privacy by doing this?

The digital world has turned our values upside down in such a way that we are almost unable to find the solutions to these problems. Digitization swept the carpet we were standing on from underneath us in an instant. A set of values, manners and etiquette that we used to be familiar with lost their meanings. Definitions triggered the change of meanings and meanings triggered the change of values. We have lost the conceptual integrity of our mental atlas. Be it our religious, ethnic or personal value judgments, the value judgments which had formed in different layers and become traditionalized started to be destroyed one by one. What is a shame, and what is not, who knows...

Although I am thinking about the effects of the digital world on our lifestyle, which is the main subject of this book, although I try to bring explanations for the reasons for our establishment of new lifestyles in my own way, I must confess that I am still having difficulty making sense of the new ways of behaving that we display. As I investigate this field, I witness with shock how Digital Schizophrenia has captured some people.

For example, the trend of sharing photos of our food on social media which has now almost become a new way of behavior... Experts say that food can satisfy a person to the extent that it appeals to five senses.[27] Apparently, people become more willing to share photos of their food when in the presence of factors beyond eating such as guessing the taste, having fun, and complementing the space with food. Unfortunately, instead of focusing on the food in a place where they are eating with their friends, the ambience surrounding them and the conversation with their friends, people are quickly taking photos of their food while it is being served before the plates have even touched the table and sharing it on social media. Besides, they are not even satisfied with having taken a photo, but they edit the image they obtained from different angles with different filters, and then share it. They are not even aware of what they are eating as they keep checking the number of likes their photos have received and having emotional ups and downs while doing this. You may have noticed that, no one knows why, there are no comments on such photo shares regarding the service of the restaurant, its menu, or the taste / seasoning of the food. Instead of comments that inform others, sharing of poetic, pun-loaded sayings has become a cliché of every social media user from all layers of society.

I am now encountering this issue while eating with various people that I know or those that I do not. When I say that I am surprised, many find it odd and mar-

---

27   Bosker, B. (2017, June 19). A Feast for the Senses. Retrieved in 2017, from http://www. newyorker.com/tech/elements/multisensory-gastronomy-a-feast-for-the-senses.

ginal. Yet it would be considered vulgar to take pride in what one eats or drinks or the amount of food one consumes on the basis of the manners of the 20th century. This means that, although I am in close contact with the digital world to the extent of conducting research on it, even I find it difficult to change some of my own behavioral codes.

The codes of etiquette have changed completely to the point we are at now. It is now a fairly common practice to share photos of our food on the internet. Still, we should not forget that this situation is completely a matter of showing-off. It is, of course, the job of psychologists and sociologists to reveal the underlying reasons for this behavior scientifically. However, it seems to me that this trend is rooted in a defense mechanism, an effort to look different. An effort to show others that they are successful and strong in life, and that life goes on with joy and good times… The motive to be the one that is envied, repair the damaged ego with comments and make disliked people jealous becomes dominant. There is actually not much difference when we compare this with the past, that is, our behaviors in the world without digital devices. People were also making efforts to become popular in social settings, just as is the case today. Just as people who went to a party, reception or meeting in the past would tell others who were not there about it in an exaggerated way, this new behavior is a virtual projection of it. People were working towards joining social settings and supporting their social statuses. The same concerns exist now in this framework. I must confess that I believe some people do not order food based on their tastes or preferences, but rather order the food they can share on social media and get the maximum number of likes with. I believe they even adjust their pose and behaviors based on this.

Regarding the values where Digital Schizophrenia is experienced in the sharpest way, it is on our agenda as an important necessity for social scientists to create new definitions and reevaluate the issue of ethics and values.

Section 5. Well, what is next?

Long Story Short

In the part of the book so far, I tried to emphasize how our lives, lifestyles and life flow have been changed by the Age of Information and the revolution related to it in the last twenty-five years, and explain how we have kept up with this on personal and social levels.

I made predictions about what could be experienced by people with low and high ICTIQ, and what could happen in issues of education, daily life, equality of opportunities, commerce, relationships and even security. While the masses that adapted to the speed of life's development utilized the opportunities, chances and benefits provided to them by this new situation, others experienced discrimination; they will continue to experience it, and be pushed out of the most basic human rights. They will wait in line for longer, not be able to find their way, miss utilizing equality of opportunities in education, and have difficulty in finding a parking space for their cars. The issue of whether it is possible to establish a mechanism that will eliminate this equality may be debated, but I believe this distance will grow even further in the future.

There may be people who will say, "when those who do not play video games or use mobile phones, namely the generation that experiences Digicrimination is gone, or in other words, when our grandparents die, the problem with communication will end, so there is no need to deal with this issue." However, as long as underdeveloped countries and low-ICTIQ people exist, we may say that this problem will persist.

Another idea is to ignore the Information and Communication technologies that surround us and impose things on us, limit their usage by Digital Detox, and even quit altogether if possible. Is it really possible? Leaving aside computers, tablets, smartphones and internet connection, is it really possible to live without TV or radio? If we refer to the famous saying by Marshall McLuhan, a fish cannot define water as it does not know about life outside it. Again, as he said, it is now possible for us to define a life without media, as it creates an environment that uses the subconscious. In short, I do not believe that an environment without bombardment by communication and media is possible.

Well, what is next? This may be our main question and problem. There are few factors that I think will change our lives in the near future and impact on our lifestyles as much as mobile phones, mobile communication and similar technologies. The instability in international relations, which has made our lives harder for the last five years with great imbalances, should be added to these.

Destruction of paper castles by international relations

Personal and social changes naturally have a dimension of politics and international relations.

The phenomenon of the Digital Ghetto may have created the most noticeable impact in these fields. Those who created a Digital Ghetto of people that are close to their ideology, view of life and political approaches did not know about and understand others, but on the contrary, they sharpened their views by creating synergy in their closed groups and became even more radical.

In an environment where value judgments are destroyed and the mass that is called *dignorant* which does not learn and stays ignorant as it thinks it can access everything in the digital environment is becoming more and more dominant, it has become easier to manipulate audiences politically. In addition to this, foreign affairs that used to operate on the basis of certain rules in the past have been carried onto more slippery ground with digitization. Secret documents or states published by the Wikileaks platform in the last few years, issues such as the e-mail scandal experienced by Hillary Clinton in the last American elections, and, though they were not taken seriously before, the claims that Russia manipulated the American presidential elections through hackers and even created an impact which was boldly mentioned by high-level officials later, have become issues that we are now seeing frequently in the news.

These scandals that erupted in international relations require that states should reevaluate their foreign relations, and discuss the activities that they conduct in the digital environment more carefully. Because of these scandals, many countries are now approaching even their relations with their past allies more carefully. The recent Brexit referendum in the United Kingdom and economic and political issues experienced in Europe are important developments that show that mutual trust has been damaged.

Another issue is the distance of political systems between the West and the East. The political imbalance seen in the Middle East with the Arab Spring that is believed to have been triggered by the power of social media, increased environment of war, violence and terror, and the wave of migration not only created great concern in Europe and even the United States, but also led to the rise of nationalist and right-wing movements by recreating the dangerous atmosphere of the 1930s. The rise in votes for far-right factions made us face as explicitly as possible the reality that issues that had been supported for years such as multiculturalism, coexistence, and respect for religion, race and ethnic backgrounds were actually paper castles. The cadres that were programmed to limit free movement to the capital and those who were like them immediately panicked and preferred closing their boundaries rather than embarking on major projects. In a way, the cards are being re-dealt in international relations with the imposition of the Age of Information, and a new order is being established.

In the international arena where relations and trust have been shaken, even though politicians show a way of behavior that stays loyal to the ethical rules established in the past, there is a serious conflict in the background. The conflict in the international arena is secretly ongoing through cyber-wars. Information sharing among countries is actually much higher in comparison with the past due to digitization. Sharing of common networks such as Interpol, security information and intelligence data is much higher than in the case of the industrial society. However, even this cooperation cannot sufficiently prevent industrial espionage. A good example is that the automotive giant Volkswagen was sanctioned by the USA as a result of incorrect declarations of the emission values of the cars they put onto the market. The revelation of the issue of the emission values actually happened through examination of the software in the cars. While activities like fraud or espionage are now easier in a digitized world, revelation of reality is equally swift and clear. As long as ethical rules are not redefined and parties do not gather around common values, it is inevitable that this chaos in personal, political and commercial relationships will continue.

Additionally, besides the issue that digital security has now undeniably become a problem in international relations, the erosion of values that had been created since the industrial society and before has now been reflected in international relations over time in addition to personal relationships. Apparently, in our time, as individuals where our personal values change and cannot be replaced with others, countries will also continue to find themselves in an environment of chaos just like individuals.

The factor that re-dealt the cards: Energy

When industrial production began with the Industrial Revolution, the issue of obtaining the energy required for production became an important problem. The infrastructure that facilitated production required high energy consumption. Reasons like the extraction of raw materials, conversion of them into products and increased heating needs due to the development of industry and urban life increased efforts to look for renewable energy sources. After the development of the industrial society, fossil fuels started to be used as sources of energy. The easiest way to produce energy was by using fossil fuels such as coal and oil. In the post-industrial era, the conversion of nuclear reactions into usable energy started to be employed as an alternate source of energy.

However, both methods of obtaining these energy resources and the usage of them created significant environmental problems. We are now experiencing environmental disasters created by advanced environmental pollution and global warming every single day.

Nature actually provides us with various alternative energy resources other than fossil fuels and nuclear energy. It is possible for us to obtain clean and constant resources through methods like wind and solar energy and water flow energy. However, long years of fossil fuel dependence and the established nature of industries based on this have prevented people from obtaining alternate energy resources.

With the information revolution, the technologies we need to utilize environment-friendly energy forms developed rapidly. Today, the cost of the technologies in question has also become affordable. The high development speed of the Information Revolution creates a domino effect and contributes to the offering of brand-new and affordable technologies on the market every day. Various sectors from automobile producers to boiler producers have structured their production on the basis of fossil fuels. This is why prominent companies in the energy sector prevented R&D operations towards environment-friendly energy resources for years. While the international lobbying activities of these companies are still going on, it is good news that many developed countries have now started promoting the use of technologies that provide clean energy. There are three charts taken from the Statista website below. They demonstrate the size of the market for solar energy and the investment made in this field. Obviously, comparative charts would make more sense when detailed reports, expert opinions and charts that are related to clean energy produced by resources like the wind are added. However, even if we did not know anything about this field, the visual message of these charts shows us how much of a leap this field has taken in such a short time. My belief is becoming stronger with the news we are following daily that this increasing trend will continue, and new upcoming lifestyles, electric cars and similar technologies will be used more frequently.

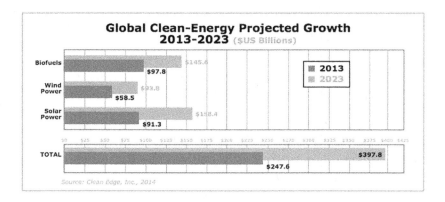

Global Clean-Energy Projected Growth
2013-2023 ($US Billions)

■ 2013	
■ 2023	

Biofuels: $145.6 / $97.8

Wind Power: $93.8 / $58.5

Solar Power: $158.4 / $91.3

TOTAL: $397.8 / $247.6

Source: Clean Edge, Inc., 2014

Statistics usage permitted by:: http://cleanedge.com/sites/default/files/PastedGraphic-1_0.png

According to the research conducted by the firm CleanEdge, the increase in the volume of the global clean energy market from 2003 to 2023 will surpass not only the increase in the conventional energy sector, but also any other conventional sector.

Again, based on studies, the capacity of solar panels set up to produce electricity between 2000 and 2015 increased almost 170-fold. The size of the billion-dollar investment that will last until 2022 by Germany, one of the countries that invest the most in non-fossil energy resources, indicates that the cards are being re-dealt in the energy field and a new market will be created. It is clear that an environment of international relations where countries that are not dependent on fossil fuels exist will be a highly different place from what has been happening for the last 150 years.

Sustainability of clean energy

The process of transition from fossil fuels to alternative energy started initially with energy resources like shale gas. Although there was awareness at this stage of development about the energy to be produced by natural resources, there were concerns about fluctuations in these resources and limited access to wind and solar energy. As technology advanced, concerns about the fluctuating reception of environmentally clean energies have diminished. Technologies that will spread energy throughout the day were created for intermittent, non-continuous energy types.

Another issue experienced in this field was the problem of storage. While electric motors were not able to create the necessary power in the past, the capabilities of electricity started to increase with new technologies. For example, an electric automobile of the past could not exceed a certain speed as it was not able to store the necessary power. This problem became history when batteries that effectively store energy were produced and a sufficient rate of storage was achieved. The functionality of electricity when it is converted to mechanical energy was also increased. The American electric car and energy company Tesla Motors is now able to produce very powerful, high-range cars with the new automobile batteries that it provides. While vehicles such as scooters and electric bikes used to be suitable for use in flat places such as the Netherlands, it is now possible to use electric vehicles in all geographical conditions thanks to the technology developed by Tesla. The prices of these technologies are also becoming more and more affordable. Some time ago, Germany stated that it will end production of cars that run on fossil fuels by the year 2030.

Some Scandinavian countries have started their work to speed up transition to electric vehicles in tractor-trailer transportation. Construction of a new highway has already started for use by these tractor-trailers that resemble the trolley buses of the past. A part of the highway named e-Highway is in operation. The construction will be finished by the year 2050.

A new lifestyle

The ongoing return to environment-friendly energy resources by various countries will bring a brand-new lifestyle onto our agenda. We will start to quit various energy resources such as gasoline or others that harm the environment and pollute it through emissions. This transformation is emerging not only in transportation vehicles but also in factories and residential complexes. New legal regulations require that all houses or buildings have batteries that will provide access to clean energy. Tesla, LG and many others have already started to produce the batteries in question that will be used at home so that the technology that will soon produce energy for an entire building via roof tiles is already on the market.

With these technologies, it will be possible to build an energy network that is self-sufficient. This will not only lead us to have increased quality of live in the environmental sense, but also eliminate the need we have for structures like gas stations. Some people working in these sectors will need to be directed towards new fields of work. We have to closely follow and analyze this rapid change in the energy sector and prepare ourselves for the future regarding employment. We need to watch out for whether this revolutionary development will create Digicrimination in the future.

Economic dependency is ending

States should be as alert as individuals regarding the widespread use of environment-friendly energies. On many occasions in the past, we witnessed how developed countries that used new technologies sent old technologies to Third World countries. In order to avoid falling into this trap, countries should make the necessary adjustments. Even countries that are considered to be very good in this matter but have not yet signed the necessary regulations for vehicles such as electric scooters and similar ones, like Germany and the Scandinavian countries, will have to take action in a short time to make the necessary changes. I think, in future times, if the fleets of a country involved in trade with, for example, Germany do not use the necessary technology, problems will be experienced in transportation and trade will be disrupted. Let us say the vehicles in your logistics fleet are still using fossil fuels, which means their entry into some regions will be prevented by new regulations. Naturally, the market share of some firms will drop if they do not adapt to the new situation. Moreover, countries that will prefer clean energy usage will get rid of their need for and economic dependency on fossil fuels. Countries that will start to utilize natural resources like wind and water while previously buying oil from abroad will achieve significant profits in the long run.

Many countries in Europe are now providing subsidies for use of nature-friendly energy. Free parking space is provided for electric cars. You can no longer find a parking space when you visit the city center with a conventional car, but you can park anywhere with an electric car. Subsidies are also provided for purchasing these vehicles. Besides, the difference in costs brought to the end user is not that much. Both individuals and states should make decisions and start implementations regarding clean energy usage in the near future.

In summary: Revolution in lifestyle by energy changes

Energy and sources of energy have been at the center of all conflicts and wars in the last 200 years. With the Information Revolution, humankind came another step closer to using natural resources such as wind and sun effectively in its energy production, and by minimizing the damage to nature. The number of firms investing in this field and seeing the future here is not one to be underestimated. While it is thought that its iconic owner Elon Musk sometimes has eccentric ideas, Tesla and similar firms have deep-rooted beliefs in the idea of ending dependency on fossil fuels using new technologies. Besides, while Tesla made a name with electric cars, the firm has also started to use batteries for the use of clean energy in homes and workplaces, and even roof tiles to produce energy from sunlight. Obviously, in line with the nature of their business, many other firms will try to follow the road taken by Tesla and take their place in this market which will become an even larger industry in the future. Despite the fact that there is a considerable number of experts claiming the opposite, I personally agree with this, too. I think the production system based on fossil fuels will be replaced by a clean energy infrastructure in a few decades. Maybe, in this context, businesses dependent on fossil fuels like gas stations will be closed down, and a new employment problem will be experienced; however, one does not have to be an oracle to say that new fields to fill this gap will emerge.

Besides the revolution that will be experienced in the transition to clean energy in terms of industrial and personal usage, relations in the international arena and conflicts about regions of power will, maybe, change direction after hundreds of years. Countries will stop being dependent on foreign powers for fossil fuels and direct their focus towards other issues.

Things are starting to speak: The Internet of Things

Every child has a favorite toy, like a doll given a name by a little girl which is almost her best friend… Sometimes, children carry their communication with these favorite toys to such a level that they treat the toy as if it is a person that actually exists. Parents are disturbed by the child creating an imaginary friend, and worry about the health of their child. In childhood, we establish a different type of communication not just with our toys, but also with everything around us. We wonder what is inside things, for example, dismantle a radio set, look inside, and try to understand what is happening. Adults also have things that they value in the same way as the little girl values her doll. These things have sentimental value for all of us.

> Phones used to be picked up only for speaking to a person who is far away. They only had one function. However, they are providing us with various opportunities of communication and entertainment. We no longer just speak with people on our phones. We are playing games, sending e-mails to take care of our business, shopping and listening to music. This situation that is called convergence is not only limited to phones, but is valid for various new things.

With the digital revolution, the communication we have had since the past is also transforming. As today's children are involved with multiple digital toys, they prefer to consume these toys instead of forming a connection with them. In addition to this, for the first time in history, objects have started to communicate with each other. Especially after smartphones entered our lives, objects have now increased their functions.

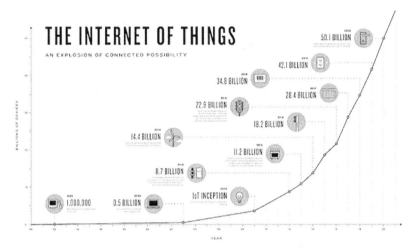

Statistics usage permitted by: https://www.hotelnewsresource.com/article85269.html

The graph above shows the increase in the number of things connected to each other. While this number was a million in 1992, it is estimated that fifty billion objects will be connected to one other by 2020. The same graph also demonstrates the difference in areas of usage for the objects.

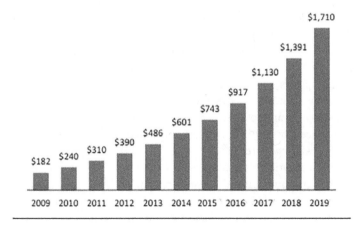

Statistics usage permitted by: http://www.hkexnews.hk/

In order to see how important this situation will become in future years, it is enough to look at what is written on the internet about predictions about the issue. According to the data of the firm HKExNews represented above, the Internet of Things market is estimated to nine-fold between 2009 and 2019.

This is an important indicator about those who are looking for a field of commercial activity.

Many different objects that are preceded by the term "smart" are now in communication with each other – for example, smart fridges. Today, with the help of the software in such a fridge, we are able to receive information on the products in our fridge that have been consumed. This software can also place orders for these products without our having the need to visit the supermarket. While these products are not actively in our lives yet, they are already a usable technology.

Nowadays, in addition to smart objects, there is also a discussion about smart cities. The days when cities may be structured in such a way that certain objects may interact with each other are upon us. For example, traffic lights placed at the side of the streets in our city will turn on and off based on the signals they receive from vehicles. Umbrellas in parks will be deployed automatically with a signal regarding the start of rain. Billboards on the side of the street we will walk by will send us notifications on our phones if the advertisement is about a thing we are interested in. With the help of software in our cars, we will find a parking spot before reaching our destination, and even be able to make payment and reserve a place. Or our car will be able to connect with the roads we are using or other cars, and let us know about the traffic status for future time intervals.

This application has already started to be used in some countries of the world. Recently, I encountered a new system in the city I live in, Hamburg. When a traffic light turned red, I started waiting as the first in line. The red light did not turn green for a long time. I was impatient, and I even thought there was a problem with the lighting system. I turned around and saw that there was a line of other cars behind me. While I was impatiently waiting, a person who was passing by approached my car and told me to drive a little further. When I did this, the red light was replaced by green. The traffic light sensed my car, understood that there was someone waiting there, and took action.

The communication that takes place between things or objects, or in my example, the communication between my car and the traffic light, is called the Internet of Things. These objects can receive signals via the data sent to a "cloud", a platform containing information on the internet from our connected devices, and perform some tasks. A different database is created on the cloud in question. These data coming from the users can, for example, detect possible transportation paths around certain points within a city. However, at this point, humankind is faced with another question: sharing personal information with everyone and failure to protect privacy. As the communication between objects increases, it is clear that there will no longer be a need to use people in many sectors. On the other hand, communication between objects is clearly not similar to communicating with a person. Many people or customers do not prefer receiving services only through devices or software. Due to these issues, the extent to which this phenomenon called the Internet of Things may be integrated into our lives is an important agenda item in the world of technology although it is still not clear. If similar implementations become abundant and assume an effective position in our daily lives, we will need to look at this concept in a more detailed way later.

Products that lead a revolution in hardware

While the Information Revolution continued to transform the traditional sectors such as education, entrepreneurship, employment, energy and marketing, it also brought brand-new fields onto our agenda. It was impossible for us to talk about a platform like social media about fifteen years ago. However, the dynamics created by the revolution in the field of software development have led to an exponential prevalence of software towards social media at first, then mobile applications, and different technological devices such as CBDs. While the focus is still on the strategic significance of software development today, we have started to see that hardware development, which fell behind software in the first years of the revolution, gained power from the speed of the revolution. While software experienced a significant launch in the first period of the revolution, we are now witnessing that the area of hardware is now increasing through devices like three-dimensional printers. Not just three-dimensional printers, but technologies like remote-controlled drones that are called unmanned aerial vehicles have now gone beyond being merely toys. Therefore, while looking at new fields introduced into our agenda by digitization, it is useful to look at developments on both the software and the hardware sides. As the internet and mobility transformed our lifestyles and allowed us to share large amounts of information easily and horizontally, it also provided a revolutionary acceleration for innovation. People who were looking for learning, innovation and invention contacted developers all around the world through the internet and found support for their work. Sometimes they just followed other's work and gained ideas about their inventions. This is how the smaller pieces of the puzzle started to come together.

Inventors before the Information Revolution were getting stuck on a problem while wanting to develop a device, and having difficulty with their work's progress. Later, they found the opportunity to gather with people with similar interests on virtual forums and share their knowledge. In this way, they started to see how they could overcome certain issues. This sharing also led to the expansion of developments on the side of hardware. Suddenly, different projects around the world started to progress fast. While this progress did not always involve significant, scientific or deep knowledge, it provided great contributions to developments in hardware in the long run.

As a result of these studies, devices and machines that we may easily use in our daily life have emerged. These inventions include "self-tying shoes", which are not that revolutionary, but we have also experienced incredible developments that overshadowed these inventions in recent years.

The 3D Printer that made our dreams come true

I am sure you too wanted to rebuild or redesign your toys, objects you liked, photographs and pictures when you were little. You must have said, "If only I had a machine to make that doll I saw on the window by myself, to create a pair of sneakers that I really like." Who could know that someone would invent the 3D printer and make our dreams come true?

The 3D printer is really a game-changer, a revolutionary product brought to us by digitization. When this product was introduced for the first time, everyone thought that this would be used only for building toys or entertainment. After the variety of its usage areas was noticed, the importance of this device was seen.

Let us say you are an astronaut and you are suddenly experiencing a malfunction in your spaceship. You need a spare part to fix a component, but you do not have time for this part to reach your ship. Right at this point, the 3D Printer comes to your help. You can now produce this device or spare part right there with the 3D Printer. This spare part I am talking about might sound too utopian, too marginal; however, think about civil society organizations that are working in remote places or hard-to-reach locations, and their needs. As long as you have electricity, this printer makes it possible to have the materials you need in an instant. This task, taken on by a 3D printer, was actually completed by Turkey's Military Academy of Medicine (GATA) as a result of hard work. They managed to produce an ear by using organic tissue. When you transfer this artificial organ to a person who needs it, it serves as a normal hearing-aid device.

The book *Homo Deus* by Yoval Harari that I mentioned before states that organ production will be the most important technological advancement that will mark our future. Harari argues that the technological gap that will form between countries in this area will explode, never to be closed again, and this will change the course of history.

The printer that challenges retailers

Of course, the production of various body parts using organic tissue is an incredible development. However, it is certain that the 3D Printer will challenge many producers commercially and affect the retail sector especially deeply. This printer supplies its user with such opportunities that there is no longer a need to go to a store and buy a spare part. Besides, it is very easy to obtain the material that is required for usage of this printer and the creation of new products. For example, plastic bottles can be easily transformed using a simple apparatus and used as 3D Printer consumables.

Such printers were not able to use metal as consumable material at first, but now there has come a point where they can even use concrete. It is a simple matter for someone to build a house in 24 hours with this technology.

Today, it is even possible to use the 3D Printer in the field of food. – that is, you can now bake a cake with this printer. All these developments indicate that various sectors from retail to food will be thoroughly shaken. This will also profoundly affect our lifestyles as users. As in the case of the period where mobile phones were first introduced, the man in the street is not greatly aware of the changes to be brought about by the 3D Printer, just as we could not imagine how much mobile phones would change our lifestyle and make it easier. We are now making the same mistake with 3D Printers. On the other hand, I cannot help mentioning that another Digicrimination cleft will form between those who embrace this technology and those who turn their backs on it. We can now see from this point that many sectors will disappear and most will be transformed on the basis of this technology.

With the increased prevalence of 3D Printers, importance will be attached to producing and presenting materials that will be used in this printer. We will also witness the birth of companies that provide support products and services such as 3D scanners and 3D modelling software. Prominent IT companies like Microsoft have already started to work on similar products that will be used in medicine and architecture. Such products are now being sold for 300–400 dollars; they are not suitable for widespread use. We can, however, see that it will be in mobile phones as an affordable application in a few years. The chart below projects that the 3D printer market will reach a volume of over 35 billion dollars in 2020. This is important as an indicator that many firms will have to go through a transformation to be part of such a large market. Many companies working in the field of photographic products faced bankruptcy as they could not predict what would happen after digital photographs and digital cameras entered the market. This is now the case for firms that are active in the field of printers.

According to research by the International Data Corporation – IDC, 3D hardware and software expenditure was about 13.2 billion dollars by 2016. Again, based on the estimation of the same organization, if the trend goes on in this way, this number will reach 29 billion in 2020.

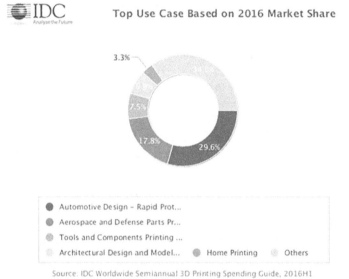

IDC
Analyze the Future

Top Use Case Based on 2016 Market Share

- Automotive Design – Rapid Prot...
- Aerospace and Defense Parts Pr...
- Tools and Components Printing ...
- Architectural Design and Model...
- Home Printing
- Others

Source: IDC Worldwide Semiannual 3D Printing Spending Guide, 2016H1

Statistic usage permitted by: www.idc.com

3D Printer usage should be taught in schools

There is a benefit in monitoring the progress of the 3D Printer and similar products in not falling into the same mistake we made about mobile phones in the past and underestimating the power of this new technology. We may see long leaps forward in this matter within the next decade. Moreover, it would not be a mistake to say that as the technologies in this field advance, some jobs will disappear. If we do not want to get caught off-guard in this issue, it would be wise for use to adopt the curricula that will teach 3D printer usage at schools from now. Just as arts classes such as music, painting and cinema are included, the subject of production with 3D Printers should also be included in the curricula.

According to a study published by *Forbes* magazine, the fields where the 3D Printer is used the most are still limited. While it is still mostly used in fields such as industrial design, concept development and product modelling, it is possible to say that this device will have a much wider scope of usage in the long run.

Drones – Unmanned Aerial Vehicles and commercial logistics

We see that, as in the case of 3D Printers, different usages for the remote-controlled flying objects that are called Drones – Unmanned Aerial Vehicles will also increase in future years. These machines were used as toys in the first few years when they were introduced on the market. Then, when it was realized that they might be used for intelligence, terrorist activities or drug smuggling, some countries started to introduce legal regulations about Drones – Unmanned Aerial Vehicles. For example, if you buy a Drone – Unmanned Aerial Vehicle in the USA, you have to get it registered with the Federal Aviation Administration.

However, a new model of usage for Drones – Unmanned Aerial Vehicles has been opened up for debate nowadays. Amazon and similar e-commerce websites that pay strategic importance to transportation by the nature of their business want to use Drones – Unmanned Aerial Vehicles for their logistic activities. It seems that this demand will open the way for various changes in the field of logistics. Drones – Unmanned Aerial Vehicles have suddenly become a product that will redefine logistics.

With their prevalence in commercial usage, there is actually no obstacle to Drones – Unmanned Aerial Vehicles becoming personal transportation/shipping tools. Besides, the video of a young man who converted his Drone – Unmanned Aerial Vehicle into a means of personal transportation started to be shared on the internet. People who see this development are trying to improve their practice. Who knows, maybe a few years later, we will not need bridges, boats, ferries or metro lines to cross the Bosphorus Strait in Istanbul.

In summary, those who thought after the Information Revolution that the lion's share was always with software are now following the developments in hardware with amazement. In fact, the revolution is rapidly impacting all areas. Small innovations come into our lives more easily, and they are able to change our lives faster and more radically.

Various studies are being conducted about the billion-dollar equivalent of the effects of Drones – Unmanned Aerial Vehicles on some sectors in 2015. Based on the findings of these studies, the one sector that caught my attention was the agriculture sector. Even the contribution these devices will make to agriculture may lead to huge changes in terms of many issues, especially regarding hunger and hormone-injected plants.

It is projected that, in the period 2015–2025 the direct influence of commercial Drones – Unmanned Aerial Vehicles on the economy of the USA will increase 5-fold. It is worth doing research about other fields that have such an effect.

Inevitable rise of hardware

To sum up, there was a consensus in the first years of the Information Revolution that hardware fell behind software. However, there are revolutionary developments happening in the area of hardware. It may be argued that affordable, accessible and multifunctional hardware gained acceleration as much as software did. One of the factors that trigger this is, of course, sharing. Inventors who experienced problems while working on a certain invention or innovation in different parts of the world started to communicate on the internet, find solutions to problems they experienced, and connect the pieces of the puzzle. This was reflected in the developments in hardware.

The 3D Printer is one of the most revolutionary products developed in the hardware field, and as I mentioned before, it is taking its place on the stage as a game-changer. With various materials used in 3D Printers including metal, plastic and concrete, we can now produce various products in food, construction, spare parts and automotives. While the current usage has focused on certain fields, it is not hard to predict that these areas will be widened greatly in the near future. Moreover, although the 3D Printer is not taken very seriously, as in the case of the first years of mobile phones, I claim that it will thoroughly shake many sectors such as the retail sector in future years, and make many professions obsolete. Likewise, Drones – Unmanned Aerial Vehicles are also going beyond toys today, and taking their place as important actors in many key sectors including shipping and agriculture. Many e-commerce companies including Amazon have already started conducting their logistic activities using Drones – Unmanned Aerial Vehicles. Even beyond this, Drones – Unmanned Aerial Vehicles will start to be used for personal transportation in addition to commercial purposes.

Another important indicator here is that, while a total of about 320,000 planes were recorded in the United States in 100 years, the number for Drones – Unmanned Aerial Vehicles was 670,000, and this is before Drones – Unmanned Aerial Vehicles have become dominant in transportation and similar areas. These are numbers that agree with my statement that digital and electronic gaps will open, never to be closed again.

The game is being reset by virtual reality

While we are not greatly aware yet, the footsteps of a brand-new revolution that will completely and uniquely change the historical progress of humankind is not so far away. This revolution will lead to a change that is far beyond what was achieved by radio and television, computers, mobile phones, and mobile communication. Virtual reality technologies are now being widely used, mostly in the corporate field or computer games. Virtual reality applications will now start to become prevalent in dating applications and sites. Whether they want a romantic relationship or sex, people will utilize virtual reality to know about the people they interact with in the virtual environment. As virtual reality technologies appeal to the five senses and therefore the emotions, they will radically influence the experience of establishing relationships in the digital environment so Such that, even though people in a relationship live in distant places, as they will find the opportunity to physically feel each other, they might not even feel the need to live in the same location in the real world. They will be able to experience their relationship in different countries and varying locations. While this does not make sense considering the relationship expectations of today, maybe it will be internalized and adopted in a short time.

Again, we will witness the real and in-depth experience of Digital Schizophrenia which I frequently mentioned in the book. What is virtual and what is real will become so intertwined that we will encounter completely different human behaviors and social communications and relationships. The biggest misconception about virtual reality today is thinking that it is limited to games and similar applications; however, as seen in the table below, virtual reality is already a great support in fields such as medicine and engineering. Telecommunications aside, in addition to economic fields like retail and shopping, virtual reality applications for pornographic content tested by the firm American Naughty at CES 2017 are indicators that another large sector will come into intense synergy with this new digital implementation. When we add fields like sports and tourism to these, it is possible to imagine what will happen.

According to estimates, in the next 5 years the billion-dollar growth of the virtual reality market will increase by more than ten times. Is this scary or is it an indicator of new opportunities?

It is expected that virtual and augmented reality applications will have a large share in fields of medicine, engineering, real estate, retail and the military in the next decade. Likewise, while not to such an extent, education will be among these fields. I think the share of education should be much more, and I believe it will be so despite current estimates.

The process of anti-socialization that is now being blamed on digital devices and applications will be carried onto another level after the real arrival of virtual reality. Because of experiences that are very close to what is real, people will give up going shopping, to movies or to sports games. A student of mine once said that maybe being anti-social is the natural state of a human, and maybe humans who gathered for reasons of hunting, shelter and security will return to their real selves for the first time in history with the help of virtual reality, and gain an opportunity to become anti-social.

Can this be true?

Number of Deals and Amount Invested in Virtual/Augmented Reality Companies Worldwide, Q1 2015-Q1 2016

	Amount invested (millions)	Number of deals
Q1 2015	$144	31
Q2 2015	$127	17
Q3 2015	$165	33
Q4 2015	$238	44
Q1 2016	$1,077	42

Note: read as $1,077 million was invested in 42 virtual/augmented reality companies during Q1 2016
Source: CB Insights as cited in company blog; eMarketer calculations, June 4, 2016
213015   www.e**Marketer**.com

Statistics usage permitted by: emarketer
https://www.emarketer.com/Chart/Number-of-Deals-Amount-Invested-VirtualAugmented-Reality-Companies-Worldwide-Q1-2015-Q1-2016/194089

The table above shows the volumes of investments and agreements in the virtual reality market in the period of 2015–2016. Numerical increase in a one-year period was 30%, while the increase in volume was 7-fold.

Conclusion

These are the good times!

The purpose of my writing this book, as I tried to explain in the beginning, was to present a profile of how electronic hardware and software have changed our lives so far and the possible effects of these geometrically increasing changes in the near future.

Based on this profile that I tried to discuss in a very concise and general sense, I aimed to talk about the change that, for me, was and is being experienced all around the world. There are several striking examples, anecdotes and references in the book; however, by starting with an example I experienced in my close circle, I wanted to describe how digital life separates us in our current position and how similar people are exposed to discrimination.

The second step was the evaluation of the definitions of concepts that come into our lives or those whose definitions change. In this section, starting with the argument that digital usage is not dependent on intelligence and a new concept is needed to assess this level of usage, I defined ICTIQ, while I defined CBD to emphasize that digital life does not consist only of computers and smartphones. Again, in this section, I discussed the reasons why I called the virtual ecosystem that people form with others who are similar to themselves or those they prefer to stay around a Digital Ghetto, by referring to an old concept. Likewise, the section where I discussed concepts like Digital Schizophrenia and Screen Addiction, and analyzed how the new digital world psychologically gets us under its influence was, again, this one.

After interpreting definitions and concepts, I listed the concepts thoroughly changed by the new digital world, especially education, and my comments about the stakeholders of these concepts. I discussed changes in commercial relationships, new factors in job applications, and issues like games, security, social media, relationships and governance in this section, and talked about the current state of affairs and the changes and developments faced in these fields.

In the last section of the book, I made predictions about the future and provided some "prophecies" about what might happen. As opposed to the cases in other sections, I used statistics and charts in this one. This way, I have visually illustrated the striking nature of the numbers. In the last section, I tried to describe the ways technologies that will come into our lives in the near future will affect us and our lives using numbers, unlike what I did in the previous sections by using examples and anecdotes.

With the synergy they created, the simultaneous leaps and changes we experienced in the 1990s in the fields of international relations, technology and communication led without any doubt to the greatest change in the history of humanity in terms of social ties. While those social ties that connected the concepts that were at the center of social definitions like economics, politics, relationships, information and communication had been reasonably renewed and tied back, after that date a mind-blowing speed took these ties and the results created by them under its influence. As I frequently repeated in the book, the revolutionary effects of the digital world on daily life and related developments in the last 25 years have overturned lifestyles in such a way that class fraction and separation, the rise of ignorance, language vulgarly used in comparison with real life, digital assault, the concept of security, generation differences, differentiation of relationships and similar social transformations have left us with an almost completely different ecology of living.

Beyond the advantages provided by digital skills in this ecology of living, I defend the idea that this is now turning into a form of discrimination in some areas of society which expects digital skills to be on a high level. Tickets that may only be bought online, job applications that may only be made online, opportunities only for academics who can give lectures in e-learning degrees… The list might be extended, but all these seem to me a new form of discrimination, rather than inequality of opportunities. This discrimination is carried out by life, the current ecology of living itself. On the other hand, this ecology has an atmosphere that is suitable for eliminating the old discrimination. That is, the masses that would refrain from gathering within the old social structure do not hesitate to gather on social media, in forums and chat rooms, and establish their own ghettos. For instance, people who would refuse to eat at the same table or travel together in real life do not mind getting together on digital platforms outside mutually held views, even by sharing opposite views. To say that Digicrimination is destroying the old discrimination may seem ambitious, but it is a correct interpretation.

As I tried to discuss in the last section of the book, the situation will not stay like this, because the developments so far have not yet created a tear in the social sense to the extent that is assumed; however, numbers and indicators show that the impositions of the digital world in the near future will make actual social discrimination and societal differentiation even greater, and make these into a gap that will never be closed again. In another perspective, my motivation while I was starting this book was the aim of creating a guide for those who are unfamiliar with issues of the Information Society, the Age of Information, informatics and related concepts. The concepts and definitions of these fields are still too technical, sophisticated and complicated for some, and thus I tried to keep the concepts, language and narrative as simple as possible and attempted to be explanatory.

As mentioned before in the book, I am not a sociologist, psychologist or a futurist. What I wrote is actually is a synthesis of the experiences I gained at Bilgi University where I taught for years, my observations, readings, what I have watched, inspirations from people around me and the things I have followed. I would like to read the future and make comments about these issues, but as explained in the book, technological developments at this point trigger each other in such different ways that providing such a prophecy, or being able to provide one, is almost impossible. It is now possible to plan on any level only through macro predictions. Despite all these there is an undeniable reality, that our future will be marked by robots, systems that can run analyses and make decisions by themselves, and by virtual reality. My claim is that everything we have defined and considered revolutionary so far will look like a drop in the ocean in comparison with these new developments I mentioned. Not everyone who cannot keep up with the new order of life will be tolerated by life as used to be the case. When there is an electronic device that does the same job more quickly, faster and cheaper, the reluctant seller will have absolutely no chance.

I would like to say and especially underline these as my last words. In the last twenty-five years, humankind has been exposed to a change that is incredibly great in terms of technology that defines and frames lifestyles. In my opinion, this change showed itself in society through the imposition of technological usage. This imposition naturally resulted in a form of discrimination. We are now on the brink of a new stage, an era where we will meet technologies that will change our lives even more than computers or smartphones have done. Hence my claim is that we will crave the difficulties we are now experiencing in terms of impositions and discriminations we have been exposed to in the last twenty-five years. In other words, these are the good times.

Sources

Adam D. I. Kramer, Jamie E. Guillory, and Jeffrey T. Hancock (2014) Experimental evidence of massive-scale emotional contagion through social networks, PNAS, Vol 111 No 24, Edited by Susan T. Fiske, Princeton University, Princeton, NJ, and approved March 25, 2014.

Andrew K.; Murayama, Kou; DeHaan, Cody R.; Gladwell, Valerie (July 2013). "Motivational, emotional, and behavioral correlates of fear of missing out". *Computers in Human Behavior.* 29: 1841–1848.

Bell, D. (1973) The Coming of Post-Industrial Society: A Venture in Social Forecasting, NY, Basic Books.

Bosker, B. (2017, June 19). A Feast for the Senses. Retrieved in 2017, from http://www.newyorker.com/tech/elements/multisensory-gastronomy-a-feast-for-the-senses.

Caillois, R. (1977). *Les jeux et les hommes: la masque et le vertige.* : Gallimard.

Damasio, A. R. (2000). *Descartes error: emotion, reason, and the human brain.* New York: Quill.

Delivery Hero Buys Middle East Web Food Service for $589 Million. (2015, May 05). Retrieved October 27, 2017, from https://www.bloomberg.com/news/articles/2015-05-05/delivery-hero-buys-middle-east-web-food-service-for-589-million

Gladwell, M. (2015). *David and Goliath underdogs, misfits, and the art of battling giants.* New York, NY: Turtleback Books.

Gonzalez, S. (2017, January 15). Meryl Streep attacks Trump in Golden Globes acceptance speech. Retrieved in 2017, from http://edition.cnn.com/2017/01/08/entertainment/meryl-streep-golden-globes-speech/index.html.

Griffith, S. B. (1982). *Sun tzu the art of war: translated and with an introduction.* London: Oxford University Press.

Harari, Y. N. (2015). *Sapiens: a brief history of humankind.* New York: Harper.

Harari, Y. N. (2016). *Homo deus: a history of tomorrow.* Toronto, Ontario: Signal.

Hill, D. (2010). *About face: the secrets of emotionally effective advertising.* London: Kogan Page.

Hilbert, M. (2012), How much information is there in the "information society"?. Significance, 9: 8–12. doi:10.1111/j.1740–9713.2012.00584.x.

How To Get Your Music Into Video Games. (n.d.). Retrieved October 29, 2017, from http://www.hypebot.com/hypebot/2011/04/advice-getting-your-music-into-video-games-.html.

Huizinga, J., & Eco, U. (2009). *Homo ludens*. Torino: Einaudi.

Isaac Asimov, (21 January 1980) "A Cult of Ignorance" Newsweek January 1980.

Joseph Steinberg (December 16, 2015). "Drones in America Must Now Be Registered. Here's What You Need to Know". *Inc.* Retrieved December 16, 2015

Lindström, M. (2010). *Buy•ology: truth and lies about why we buy*. New York: Broadway Books.

Lindström, M. (2010). *Brand sense: build powerful brands through touch, taste, smell, sight and sound*. London: Kogan Page.

Loader, B. D. (2006). *Cyberspace divide: equality, agency and policy in the information society*. London: Routledge.

Madrid, B. C. (1981, February 23). King Orders army to crush coup. Retrieved October 29, 2017, from https://www.theguardian.com/world/1981/feb/23/spain.fromthearchive.

Orwell, G. (2016). *1984*. Lexington, KY: Publisher not identified.

Roger Bohn and James E. Short (2012), Measuring Consumer Information, International Journal of Communication 6, 980–1000.

Tamir, D.I., & Mitchell, J.P. (2012). Disclosing information about the self is intrinsically rewarding. Procedings of the National Academy of Sciences, 109 (21), 8038–8043.doi:10.1073/pnas.1202129109.

Toffler, A. (1980). *The third wave*. New York: William Morrow.

U.S. Department of Commerce, National Telecommunications and Information Administration (NTIA). (1995). *Falling through the net: A survey of the have nots in rural and urban America*. Retrieved from, http://www.ntia.doc.gov/ntiahome/fallingthru.html.

Graphics and webpages

2045 Initiative http://www.2045.com

Adweek Infographic: World Cup Shatters Facebook Engagement Records. (n.d.). Retrieved in 2017, from http://www.adweek.com/lostremote/infographic-world-cup-shatters-facebook-engagement-records/46217

Asgardia https://asgardia.space/en/

Cleanedge: Global Clean Energy projected grown: Retrieved in 2017 from http://cleanedge.com/sites/default/files/PastedGraphic-1_0.png

Emarketer : Network Users Penetration; Retrieved in 2017 from https://www.emarketer.com/Chart/Social-Network-Users-Penetration-Worldwide-2014-2020-billions-change-of-internet-users/190584

Emarketer: Number of Deals Amount Invested Virtual Augmented Reality Companies Worldwide Q1-2015-Q1-2016: Retrieved in 2017 from https://www.emarketer.com/Chart/Number-of-Deals-Amount-Invested-VirtualAugmented-Reality-Companies-Worldwide-Q1-2015-Q1-2016/194089

HKexNews: The Internet of Things Market: Retrieved in 2017 from http://www.hkexnews.hk/

Hotelnews Resources: an Explosion of Connected Possibilities: Retrieved in 2017 from https://www.hotelnewsresource.com/article85269.html

IDC: Top use cased of 3D printers; Retrieved in 2017 from www.idc.com

Login Radius Infographic: The Global Sharing Popularity: Retrieved in 2017 from https://2yu5yy2vwpsr4dg1ys3jha9o-wpengine.netdna-ssl.com/wp-content/uploads/2016/04/2016_Q1_Social-Sharing-Global-Popularity.png